BUILDING WITH
FRANK LLOYD WRIGHT

Massive stonework frames one side of the stairway in the solar hemicycle, third house designed by Frank Lloyd Wright for the Jacobs family. With a deceptively simple curve and unusual skylighting, Wright transformed the utilitarian stairs to the five-bedroom mezzanine into a dramatic area of the house. (Photo © Ezra Stoller)

BUILDING WITH FRANK LLOYD WRIGHT

AN ILLUSTRATED MEMOIR

BY HERBERT JACOBS with Katherine Jacobs

Published in association with ROBERT BRIGGS

CHRONICLE BOOKS • SAN FRANCISCO • A PRISM EDITION

The letters and drawings of Frank Lloyd Wright are owned and copyrighted by the Frank Lloyd Wright Foundation; the letter of Olgivanna Lloyd Wright is owned and copyrighted by Olgivanna Lloyd Wright.

Part of this book is derived from research conducted under a grant to the author from the National Endowment for the Arts in Washington, D.C., a Federal agency.

Some of the material published here was made available through the courtesy of the Burnham Architectural Library of the Art Institute of Chicago, which houses the Herbert and Katherine Jacobs Collection.

Cover photo by Jack Steinberg: "Stonework for the Solar Hemicycle"

Library of Congress Cataloging in Publication Data

Jacobs, Herbert Austin.
  Building with Frank Lloyd Wright.

  "A Prism edition."
  Includes index.
  1. Wright, Frank Lloyd, 1867-1959.
I. Jacobs, Katherine, joint author. II. Title.

NA737.W7J32   728.6'4   78-27520
ISBN 0-87701-126-5
ISBN 0-87701-127-3 pbk.

Contents

ALSO BY HERBERT JACOBS

We Chose the Country
The Try and Stump Me Yearbook
A Practical Guide for the Beginning Farmer
The Community Newspaper
Practical Publicity
Frank Lloyd Wright: America's Greatest Architect

Acknowledgments

I am indebted to Donald G. Kalec, associate professor, School of Art, Art Institute of Chicago and director of the Research Center of the Frank Lloyd Wright Home and Studio Foundation, Oak Park, Illinois, for checking the accuracy of architectural and other matters; to Edgar Tafel, New York architect, author of *Apprentice to Genius* and friend since my earliest visit to Taliesin, for encouraging and facilitating my application for a grant from the National Endowment for the Arts which resulted in assembling a mass of material from which much of this book was drawn; and to John Zukowsky, architectural archivist of the Burnham Architectural Library, Art Institute of Chicago, where the collection is housed.

Thanks also are due for pictures, negatives, drawings and letters made available by Lawrence Cuneo, the Frank Lloyd Wright Foundation, Pedro E. Guerrero, James Roy Miller, John Sergeant, Mrs. Jack Steinberg, Ezra Stoller, Carmie A. Thompson, Time, Inc. and the Whitney Library of Design. And a special thanks to my editor, Susan Harper, for sympathetic attention to the form and coherence of the manuscript.

Herbert Jacobs

Introduction

By Karel Yasko

(Fellow, American Institute of Architects, ASCE, and former Wisconsin State Architect)

At last, an architect's client speaks up and out, and tells "how it was" to build not one, but two Frank Lloyd Wright houses. And these were not ordinary houses, even by Mr. Wright's standards! The first was in response to a challenge to "design us a decent house to cost not more than $5,000" (even in 1936 that was cheap). The second was to be low-cost though larger, and not completed until eleven years later.

Both objectives were achieved through a series of remarkable experiences, detailed in the following pages by a client and his wife who were articulate, sympathetic yet not uncritical, and possessed of great determination. Architects, building contractors, and especially all persons building or thinking of building can profit from a story told here with verve, humor and engrossing detail. Architect Wright's reputation will gain another notch, and the equally remarkable clients, Herb and Katherine Jacobs, were obviously delighted.

My first view of Usonia No. I, as Wright called the low-cost Jacobs house, was under cover of darkness, the night after the carport support post had been knocked out by the driverless car of a neighbor which had slipped its brake and charged across the street. There was the gallant roof, partly supported on the inner right angle where it touched the building—and it was without a wiggle. A Wisconsin snow might have bent it a bit, but could not break it.

It was a good introduction to my first Frank Lloyd Wright house.

Not that I wasn't familiar with Mr. Wright's structures. In architectural school in the mid-thirties I had pondered every one of the published versions. For two years my student projects were all Wrightian, no matter what the building was. I had gone from sneering to cheering, after a Wright admirer, an upperclassman whom I respected, pointed the way from Beaux Arts to the cheering section. He told me I'd soon become an addict.

My first after-school job was at the College of William and Mary, and one of the chores was to write column-length press stories for the school's forthcoming comprehensive exhibition of Frank Lloyd Wright's work. It was the first in the U.S., and inspired the subsequent show at the Museum of Modern Art in New York. To prepare the stories I again read all Mr. Wright's writings and exchanged a series of letters with him; so I had the words and thoughts to prepare the citizens of Virginia.

Mr. Wright was wined and dined before his opening night's talk. Some of the dinner guests had their suspicions of his eccentricities confirmed when, after dinner, we were preparing to walk from the inn to the lecture hall. Mr. Wright and I were discussing his design for the "morning glory" columns to support the roof of the Johnson Administration Building, in Racine, Wisconsin, when Wright suddenly leaped into the air with both feet together like a ballet dancer, to show me how the structural force concentration worked. The awed silence of the onlookers was an impressive tribute to his agility, since he was then about seventy years old.

Still, I was impressed by that carport roof on that first visit. Now came the great moment of entry to the five thousand dollar Usonian house. We were not the paying tourists who still came in droves; I deadheaded as a professional courtesy and my architect escort was a friend of Herb and Katherine. It was the first of several visits, which I made every time I could get away from my nearby construction job.

My first impression, after a tour of the house with the Jacobses—who had the visitor routine down pat, including the answers to the standard questions—was that it was a simple yet complex living house. You were allowed to be yourself, but at the same time the house was subtly influencing and changing you. Winston Churchill said something later to the effect that we first shape a building and then the building shapes us. Thus when Mr. Wright spoke of designing individual houses for the individual family he was only partly accurate. He really meant that he was providing an individual environment which would shape the fami-

ly to it. In this case it worked so well that one of the children later became a member of the Taliesin Fellowship.

I kept at Herb on that first tour. "You do mean it cost only five thousand dollars?" "No," said he, "five thousand five hundred," and he explained that the extra amount came because they added a third bedroom.

And there were structural questions. We tend to take as a matter of course now the many structural innovations of the Jacobs house because so many of them have been incorporated for years into the mainstream of American home construction (for instance, carport, floor heating, corner windows, grouping of utilities in a central stack, a concrete mat, and patterned walls) but they were new then. The planning grid (today called modular construction, as if it were a new discovery) was apparent to my trained eye, so I asked no questions about it. "The exterior wall is so thin," I remember commenting. "And the entire house is heated through this warm concrete floor?" I added. "Yuph," was the reply.

But I would not let go of the heating system idea: the possibilities for a home were so intriguing. As Herb described it, the piping was laid directly on the gravel bed, more than half buried in it, and the concrete mat laid on top. Several years later I discovered that Wright used the same heating system in the Charles Manson house of 1941, in Wausau, Wisconsin—a house where I was to spend much time recuperating in the tower room.

I learned from both installations when my time came to design a system in cold Wausau. The two houses bear some other comparisons. The Jacobs house cost fifty-five hundred dollars and apparently didn't bankrupt the contractor. The Manson house, built a few years later and slightly larger, cost thirteen thousand, and the contractor said later that he had "wanted the experience," and that no other contractor in the area would even look at the plans. The siting of the Jacobs house on the lot, established by Wright, who designed to it superbly, was also better than that for Manson. The interiors of both houses were Frank Lloyd Wright at his best in simple, direct spaces without strong planes slicing into them.

Both Herb and Katherine, properly shaped by Mr. Wright, after five years in their Usonian house and then six years in an old farmhouse, were ready for another house. This time the challenge was the site. The house was to be low-cost with a few amenities (the plunge pool); the Jacobses were going to be very active participants in the construction. (Still-calloused hands typed the story about it.)

Mr. Wright was ready with his solar hemicycle, built five years after its design (because of the war-time interval). There was no similarity to the Usonian concept. Here Mr. Wright used the earth instead of blank walls against the north wind and for privacy. Gone are the sharp angles of the plan; instead, a flowing single space reaching out to embrace the garden and to gather in the solar energy production with a bosom of glass. Into the space were hung the sleeping quarters treated like temporary intruders—no doors and depending on the main single floor heating system. Entry to this great single room is through a tunnel through the earth berm—quiet, simple and low key—and you're in a great dazzling sunlighted and sun-heated curved flowing space. It is THE experience.

The complex design was made simple in the drawing delineation, so that nonprofessionals could build it without compromise and with absolutely minimal direction or interpretation from the designer. Materials, forms and spaces came together like clockwork. And the result should be discovered today by the energy conservationists. It would obviate their energy in reinventing what Mr. Wright already did in this house over thirty years ago.

Later when I became State Architect for Wisconsin it was my dream to have a state facility from the hand of Frank Lloyd Wright. As he grew older he was "discovering architecture," he told me. While I was searching for the appropriate project and softening up the very skeptical officials, Mr. Wright's time was running out, though I thought he would go on forever. A state building would have been an official recognition of the state's most creative offspring and would have made amends for the long, bitter attacks on him. But he couldn't wait.

Still, there has to be a great tribute to Herb and Katherine Jacobs as well as to Frank Lloyd Wright in both of the Jacobs houses, though perhaps greater in the second.

Part One

USONIA NUMBER ONE

I.

A Challenge
Tossed Back

We first met Frank Lloyd Wright on a warm August afternoon in 1936, when one of his twenty architectural apprentices led us through a maze of slant-topped drafting desks to where the architect was sitting. He rose to greet us, erect and making the most of his five feet eight-and-a-half inches of height—"Had I been taller," he had once declared, "all my buildings probably would have been proportionately higher." His abundant iron-gray hair was carefully brushed back from his forehead, his handshake firm, his smile warm as his twinkling eyes sized us up. He made us feel at ease while I stammered out our question of whether he could design "a decent five-thousand-dollar house" for us.

"Would you really be satisfied with a five-thousand-dollar house?" he countered. "Most people want a ten-thousand-dollar house for five thousand dollars." He waited, smiling, to let that shaft sink in, as we hastened to assure him that "of course" we realized that it did not need to be fancy.

At this point Wright said in the quizzical, half-teasing manner which often masked his serious concern, " 'Will you walk into my parlor?' said the spider to the fly," and led the way into his private office behind the drafting room, whose windows looked out over miles of Wisconsin River valley to the mauve-tinted bluffs which edged it in the distance. We were about to be caught up in a delightful web of architecture which lasted more than forty years. And for twenty-five of those years I would be his friend and chief newspaper chronicler, as well as client.

The question of how we happened to meet Wright came later from friends as well as strangers, when they learned that he designed three moderate-cost houses for us and that we built and lived in two of them for twenty years. Their eyebrows usually rose further when they discovered that we had virtually no money while dealing with this "architect of millionaires."

To our astonishment—and sometimes inconvenience—the two houses we built became world famous architecturally, because both were highly innovative pioneering structures in the moderate-cost housing field, though builders did not fully grasp their lessons. A Swiss architectural magazine editor has called them "the best prototypes of true environmental houses." We believe their story is worth telling at some length because they give important pointers to economies in an industry plagued by high costs, partly the result of inflated, unthinking demands of clients offered no reasonable alternatives.

So how did this meeting with Wright come about? A series of coincidences, among them the Great Depression of the 1930s, combined not only to lead us to Wright, but to make the construction possible. Katherine and I, then with one small daughter, had been living on a newspaperman's very modest salary (just twenty dollars a week at the time of our marriage, with no such thing as overtime pay). A sudden opportunity came, in the early summer of 1936, to move from Milwaukee to what seemed like a job with better prospects in the capital city of Madison, Wisconsin. And we thought we needed a better house than we found available for rent in Madison.

In both Madison and Milwaukee we had seen a few examples of the whitewashed austerities of the International Style, which at that time passed as modern architecture, but we were not attracted. Like most young people we were full of prejudices, ignorance and misinformation on what a house should be, and had no conception of how good architecture could mold and greatly enhance a way of living.

Then Harold Wescott, an artist cousin of Katherine's, said, "Why not build your own house in Madison, and have Frank Lloyd Wright design it for you?" He had recently spent a summer at Taliesin, Wright's studio-home near Spring Green, Wisconsin, just forty miles west of Madison, and had become a Wright enthusiast. We were dubious, sure that the famous man would not care to trouble himself with our small needs, but Harold insisted on making an appointment for us to see Wright.

When Katherine and I set out from Madison on that humid August afternoon we talked over possible ways of tempting

Wright to do something for us. We thought perhaps a bold challenge might stir him, so we decided to say, "What this country needs is a decent five-thousand-dollar-house. Can you build it?" Before you laugh in disbelief at that small sum, let me remind you that prices were indeed low in those Depression days. Only a couple of years before, as an all-night police reporter, I usually ate my main meal of the day, which of course was after midnight, at a downtown restaurant which sported a big sign in the window: "Two eggs, any style, 5 cents. Limit 8 to a customer." You could get a stack of three slices of buttered toast for another five cents. A cup of coffee also cost just a nickel.

The Depression itself was a major element in our seeking out Wright. As a recently married couple we had participated with friends several times, at both formal and informal meetings, in the favorite Depression game of "When we have money enough to build a house we'll---" and so on, with hour after hour of rambling discussion. In Sunday walks around our middle-class Milwaukee suburban area we picked out housing styles that we liked, and decided that a "modified Dutch colonial" of white-painted brick was our *beau ideal*. But when we asked Harold Wescott what sort of house we might get from Wright he sketched a simpler plan than conventional houses of the day, with a living room wide open to a garden and incorporating a dining area and large fireplace. The plan attracted Katherine, but left me cold to the point of uneasy chill. All I murmured aloud, however, was something like "Remarkable! Very interesting."

When we arrived at Taliesin, which means "shining brow" in Wright's ancestral Welsh and is also the name of a Welsh third-century bard, we walked hesitantly up the limestone steps, staring at the rough stonework of the low buildings which clustered on three sides of a central courtyard. One of the apprentices passing through the courtyard asked us to wait while he informed Mr. Wright that we had arrived. We continued to inspect the stonework, the unusual casement windows, the low eaves of one building which almost reached the ground. The wood and stone, the close relation to the ground, seemed warm and real, and suited to our modest way of life.

On a later visit we discovered the small square hatchway in the ceiling of the entryway which showed the charred underside of roof boards. This grim reminder marked the farthest point of a disastrous fire that destroyed much of Taliesin in 1925—the second time that Taliesin had been hit by such a holocaust.

After we were seated in Wright's office he told us that for twenty years he had wanted to design a low-cost house and had been pondering many ideas; but we were the first clients who had ever asked him for such a design, he said. Then he ticked off some of the things that we would have to do without. A tiled bathroom, expensive interior cabinet work, and elaborate construction would be among the casualties. We did not blanch at the prospect, since neither of us had ever experienced such luxuries, and in fact had not even dreamed of them. We both came of parents of modest means who were strong on education and a pioneering attitude. Katherine had been born and grew up on a small farm in the kettle moraine country of Wisconsin, and was the youngest of six children. I was one of four children of college-educated, pioneering social worker parents, who ran a social settlement house in a Polish factory workers' neighborhood on Milwaukee's South Side.

It soon developed that the most startling innovation that Wright wanted to introduce into our proposed house was what he then called "holocaust heating." In the four years he had spent in Japan directing the building of the Imperial Hotel in Tokyo—one of a handful of major buildings to survive the gigantic earthquake and fire of 1923—he had become familiar with the system used for centuries by Koreans, who kept floor and house warm by winding the smoke from a small fire through a maze of hollow tiles under the floor before the smoke reached the chimney. All previous clients had shied away from the proposal. He pointed out that this kind of heating did away with expensive and space-consuming radiators or hot-air ducts, and produced draftless, even temperatures throughout. Ours would be the first residence in America to have such a system, he declared.

We said the idea seemed eminently sensible and logical, and we would probably be willing to try it. I believe that Wright felt there and then that here were clients who might well stay the course. We did not know that Wright planned to use this system, which he at first called radiant heat, and later gravity heat, in the great H.C. Johnson and Son Company's administration building, the com-

Flanked by a few Japanese prints from his enormous collection, and with architectural T-square and pencils before him, Frank Lloyd Wright sits at ease at the desk in his private office as he chats with a visitor. Sometimes for relaxation he played the small organ which shows behind his chair. (Photo by James Roy Miller)

mission for which he had received just weeks before. Since our house would likely be completed long before the Johnson building, it would give Wright a chance to experiment, and reassure Johnson that the system would really work.

I don't know that we were swept off our feet—maybe one toe still stayed on the ground—but we certainly were enchanted by his persuasiveness, to the point where we were about ready to accept almost anything that he prescribed. We drove back to Madison debating all the way, and spent the next days continuing the discussion and counting pennies. Wright had told us he could do nothing until we had some land.

Starting almost immediately, I began peppering Wright with letters and memos, in the brash manner that comes naturally to

newspapermen, beseeching him for speed or more economy, or making suggestions. Within a week I wrote, on the common newsprint we used at the paper for stories: "My wife and I are still agreed that we would be satisfied with a $5,000 house—provided that you are its architect . . . I hope that you can take time from your other work to open a door for us." And then I added, with all the innocence of the ignorant: "Perhaps $5,000 is not the best figure to be mentioning so often, since I estimate that sum must include both house and lot. Since talking to you, however, we have concluded that we can do very well on two bedrooms instead of three, and are already pruning down a list of what at first seemed absolute essentials." I even added that of course we expected to be living in the house within three months.

Obviously we were grossly naive about building practices, as evidenced by the comment that the proposed five thousand dollars "must include both house and lot." The prospective owner may think of house and lot, utilities, landscaping, and even furniture, as making up the total sum he can commit, but surely Wright was in this instance like many another architect: he considered the whole amount as barely sufficient just for the shell he would be designing. If the architect considered cost of land, landscaping, and the inevitable other items like heating, furniture and decoration, the building he designed would be so small as to risk rejection by the client. Wright avoided some of these additional costs by the simplicity of his designs (at least for lower-cost houses) and the provision for building-in much of the furniture.

He never mentioned the statement that the five thousand dollars had to include land and everything else. He apparently decided to let that one slide, to give us time to educate ourselves about the realities. A less patient and understanding man might have been offended at some of my bristling comments then and later, but instead he was highly amused, I learned many years later from an architect friend who frequently visited Taliesin at that time.

Another splendid example of our naiveté revealed itself in our expectation of having the working drawings and all construction completed before the Taliesinites left in mid-November for their annual winter in Arizona. As it turned out, it would be over a year before we moved into the house—still uncompleted. Later we saw many examples of people who did manage to order a house from a contractor and get it built within three months, sometimes, giving them plenty of time in the dreary years ahead to repent their haste.

We thought Wright or "somebody from Taliesin" would help us pick out a building site, but the architect was too busy, and probably too wary, to get into that kind of tangled thicket. Being newspaper-oriented, we looked in the want ads for building lots that we thought were in our price range. One lot owner, P.B. "Bert" Grove, who said he was a builder, solemnly declared, "I'd give my right arm to build a building by Wright." We thought this showed real dedication, rather than calculated salesmanship. Although we did not buy his lot, he eventually did become the

contractor; we did not know until later that he had no work crew, and actually subcontracted all the work to other small builders. But he did do a fair job, with Wright breathing down his neck all the time.

We finally picked a lot in a virtually undeveloped suburban tract called Westmorland, at the west end of Madison, just two outside the city limits. About twenty houses stood scattered over the quarter-mile area of the tract. The streets had narrow paving of aging concrete, with elms along them. Hay grew, and was being cut, on most of the hundreds of unsold lots. The area had been laid out just before the Depression, and all the lots had pipes for water and gas, but not for sewers. The lot we bought was 60 feet wide and 120 feet deep, and it cost us eight hundred dollars.

That money represented just about half of our total capital, and it had come, unexpectedly but delightfully, as a windfall inheritance from a great-aunt of mine who had died some years before in Los Angeles. Her money was tied up in Los Angeles real estate, and actual sale did not come until the depths of the Depression, drastically cutting the value.

But the economic situation had other aspects which did work in our favor. Building materials were cheap, and so was mortgage money. A pool of skilled craftsmen stood willing to work at low wages. President Roosevelt's New Deal Administrators, desperately anxious to create jobs, had set up the Federal Housing Administration to stimulate construction, and its agents were virtually peddling mortgage money in the streets. They would certainly finance us, everyone declared.

It had not occurred to us, when I wrote Wright that we hoped he would find time for us from his other clients, that he had just been through half a dozen very lean years. He had been jobless on a grand scale because of the overhead involved in his elaborate studio-home, but prospective clients either had no money available, or were frightened off by Wright's much-publicized marital and legal difficulties.

In 1932, with no clients in sight, Wright had boldly struck out with a new venture, creating the Taliesin Fellowship of twenty young men and women who would live at Taliesin as apprentices in architecture. They were devoted enthusiasts, inspired by Wright's lectures, and with parents willing to pay the yearly fee (at

A giant oak tree, supporting a big Japanese temple bell, enclosed one side of the courtyard at Taliesin, Wright's studio-home. The rough stone of the buildings typified Wright's use of natural materials and the low, sloping roofs, relating buildings to site, introduced prospective clients and visitors to the special world that Wright presided over. The young apprentices gathered frequently on stone seats under the oak for the afternoon tea break, and this was also the assembly place for guests at Taliesin parties. (Photo by Carmie A. Thompson)

This "abstract forest," as Wright called it, of oak trusses and beams supported the roof of the big drafting room at Taliesin. The architect calculated the shrinkage of the green oak so exactly that the beams fitted perfectly after they dried, and lasted more than forty years before some needed replacement. Drawings and perspectives of Wright buildings were hung on the walls where clients could examine them and models of some of the structures were placed nearby. (Photo by Herbert Jacobs)

first $650, but soon raised to $1,100) for the privilege of working under the direction of the master. And work they did. The Taliesin buildings desperately needed repairs, as well as additions. Each apprentice was required to come armed with a hammer and saw, and they got plenty of use. The youths quarried their own stone, and learned to lay it up in walls with mortar made from lime they produced by burning limestone in the Taliesin kiln. Carpentering, plastering, steam-fitting and plumbing were other skills gradually learned, because Wright believed an architect could design a better wall, for instance, if he knew the skill it took to lay one up. They also got abundant doses of gardening, since Taliesin had to raise, and can for winter, most of its own food. The apprentices took their turns at cooking, table decoration, serving and entertainment of guests—important background for the more creative work at drafting boards.

Wright had designed a huge new drafting room, with sleeping quarters in small rooms along its sides for the apprentices, and they and some hired help built it from green oak boards sawed on the job. Nearly as good an engineer as architect, Wright had

calculated the shrinkages of the green lumber so exactly that the great wooden trusses which span the roof—he called them an abstract forest—fitted perfectly when they dried in place.

Theoretically, the apprentices would also assist Wright in his architectural work, acting as draftsmen under his direction, in drawing plans for clients. But there weren't any clients. The first sizeable comissions in many a long year were for the Johnson administration building, and the spectacular Kaufmann house, Fallingwater, commissioned in 1935 for the Pittsburgh department store magnate whose son had spent some time as a Taliesin apprentice.

I was already slightly familiar with Taliesin and Wright's apprentice fellowship because the *Milwaukee Journal* had sent me out in November, 1934, just two years after establishment of the fellowship, to do a progress report on how they were getting on. I was so ignorant of Wright and the whole subject of architecture then, and so unused to the need for advance preparation, that I did not bother to look in the newspaper's library for clippings which would have helped me to ask more intelligent questions. I simply called and made an appointment with Wright for a few days later.

But I had other things on my mind right then. The birth of our first child impended, and I took Katherine to the hospital the evening before I was slated to interview Wright. However, the "early signs and tokens" of labor subsided instead of increasing. The nurses finally gave me a bed in the maternity ward, and shoved me off at dawn with the assurance that nothing would happen that day.

Since the paper did not even think it worthwhile to send along a photographer, I drove alone the hundred and twenty miles through a chill and gray Wisconsin countryside. I arrived at Taliesin just as Wright was about to leave to set up a small architectural exhibit at Dodgeville, twenty miles away. He had forgotten all about my appointment, a not infrequent failing of his. A few years later Gus Pabst, then the prestigious financial editor of the *Journal*—he sometimes appeared Saturday night at the office in jodhpurs and boots, fresh from the polo field, to check over his financial pages—drove out to Taliesin for an appointment with Wright, only to find that the great man had gone to the dentist. Pabst, a man unaccustomed to waiting, cooled his heels for more than two hours. Finally made aware by the bustling of apprentices that Wright had returned, Pabst inquired about his appointment. He was told that the master was killing flies—a diversion which was such a favorite of Wright's that apprentices frequently gave him gaily decorated flyswatters. At this news the seething Pabst stormed out, but calmed down enough at his office to write an amusing and light-hearted account of his near-interview.

Since I was a much lesser light at the *Journal* than Pabst, I had no option but to hang onto Wright as long as I could, which turned out to be a little over ten minutes. He was wearing baggy pants of his own design, gathered at the ankle, with a long woolen scarf wrapped around his neck, and a floppy French beret atop his head. The beret kept falling forward over his eyes as he spoke, and Wright would solemnly lift the fabric by its tiny tassel and settle it farther back on his head. Soon he left abruptly, saying, "Some of the boys will talk to you now."

The boys were rather long-haired, smiling and polite young men, bundled up in sweaters and scarves, with stocking caps pulled down on their heads, because Taliesin was trying to make do with open fireplaces for heat. Two of them took me half a mile across the fields to show off the new drafting room being finished near Hillside. Wright had designed the Hillside cluster of buildings some thirty-five years earlier to house a private school run by two of his aunts in the valley where almost every farm was occupied by his Welsh relatives. The two apprentices, "Bob" Mosher (he never used his give name, Byron Keeler Mosher) and Edgar Tafel, who later became our good friends and went on to successful architecture careers away from Taliesin, tried to explain to my uncomprehending ears what Wright meant when he talked of his architecture as being "organic." Finally, when I had exhausted their patience, I started back to Milwaukee, learning on the way through a telephone call to the hospital that I had become a father at about eleven o'clock that morning, at the very moment I was interviewing Wright. I thought I saw a small smile on the face of the new daughter that night when I looked at her behind the glass at the hospital, but it was probably just due to a gas bubble. Perhaps she would have laughed out loud, as I certainly would have, if I had been told then that we would later live in two Wright houses, and that she would join the Taliesin Fellowship, where she became a leading figure in the musical, dance and graphics aspects of their life.

The Taliesin visit of two years earlier was scarcely in my thoughts that steaming late-August of 1936 in Madison as Katherine and I drew up a whole list of questions and "absolute requirements" we intended to hand to Wright. We had been invited to dinner there, and we were determined that while he was putting those lines on drafting paper he should have some firm guidelines beside him. That now tattered and yellowed sheet of newsprint, of which I kept a carbon, shows that we were still living in a highly conventional world rather than envisioning anything of Wright's organic architectural ambience. But we were certainly thinking economically. We did cut our requirements to two bedrooms instead of three, but declared that "provision should be made for future additions of bedrooms, to allow for increase in family." We even suggested a screen in a corner of the living room as a sufficient provision for guest space.

Far from wall-to-wall carpeting, our only suggestion for a floor covering was "tiling or linoleum on end of living room used for dining," and linoleum in the small bedroom for the child. (Years later, when we felt we could afford some kind of carpeting, Wright declared that children should enjoy the same comforts as their parents. He sketched a carpet layout that carried from the living room past the dining area and into halls and bedrooms, leaving bare floor over most of the heating pipes. We bought a bolt of cheap felt carpeting, and cut it up ourselves.)

"Plenty of closet space," we demanded in the familiar cry, and "kitchen and bathroom fixtures should be hung high," because we were both tall, and already tired of stooping. I specified that no ceiling in the house should be lower than six feet six inches, because I had heard that Wright often designed ceilings at six feet four inches. I was a bit over six feet, and I told Wright jocularly at one point, "I want to be able to wear my hat anywhere in the house, including the bedroom."

After the Taliesin dinner we went again with Wright to the drafting room, where we thought we would be discussing our list of housing requirements, given to him on our arrival. But the list was never mentioned. Wright was delighted that we were willing to go along with his idea of heating through the floor, but said it probably would be done with steam pipes rather than a meandering maze of tiles with smoke going through them. "Too cold in Wisconsin for that to be effective," he said.

He then launched into a discussion of the innovations he planned for a house of moderate cost. The house would be covered with a flat roof, letting the water run off at the sides, and avoiding gutters and downspouts as needless expense. Visible, pitched roofs are unnecessary and expensive, especially when they are "ruffled by a hip or valley or dormer," he declared. That meant no attic, one of Wright's abominations because it was just used to hang onto junk, he said. Grouping of utilities to permit short runs of pipe would be another economy. Wiring of the house would be simplified to make the wiring itself the light fixtures, reflecting light from the ceiling. Heating through the floor would eliminate radiators, which would take up wall space and collect dirt.

Wright declared that we would not need any expensive furniture, because most of it would be built-in as part of the house. Instead of an enclosed garage he proposed a carport, a new word and new idea then, with walls merely on two sides, and an overhanging roof. "A car is not a horse, and it doesn't need a barn," Wright said. "Cars are built well enough now so that they do not need elaborate shelter." We had no trouble going all the way with him there. Our cheap secondhand car had stood out all winter at the curb, often in weather far below zero. A carport would be a downright luxury for it.

The architect proposed a novel kind of "sandwich" wall, built without the conventional studding framework: just three thicknesses of one-inch boards held in place by battens, and with building paper between them. This solid wall would be both fire- and vermin-resistant, and would eliminate the need for plastering or painting, Wright declared. He added an over-simplified statement that later came back to haunt him: "Wood best preserves itself." (Several months after we had been installed in the house he said a coating of linseed oil on the outside would be "a good idea" to preserve the wood.)

The "architect of millionaires" was showing himself very economy-minded indeed. He called the designing of a moderate-cost house "America's major architectural problem" and declared that in choosing a house with the innovations and economies he described we would not only be benefitting ourselves, but pointing out an economical path for others. When we left, digesting ideas that we felt seemed so sensible, we went off as crusaders, fired with enthusiasm. And as we left, Wright promised to have some plans to show us "soon."

At only one point did we balk. Wright suggested that we would be better off to build in the country, rather than on a city lot, but we declined. It took five years of living at the edge of the city before we came around, independently, to his point of view.

2.

The Backward House

"This house turns its back on the street," Wright told us with a smile of immense satisfaction, and Katherine and I smiled back, not really comprehending, and waited to hear more as he spread out the floor plan before us. In fact, I don't think we grasped the full implications of this violent break with American middle-class housing concepts until years later.

We had come for the third time to Taliesin, in mid-September, 1936, in response to a note from Eugene Masselink, Wright's secretary, saying that Mr. Wright was ready to see us now concerning our house and he suggested that we come out for dinner sometime that week—any time that suited us. We were still confidently expecting to be in our new home before Christmas, and we hurried right out to Taliesin.

Wright must have been amused at our gross ignorance of all that is involved in design and building, but he was the soul of consideration—gentle, explanatory, persuasive, inspirational. At that time, before the rush of clients which followed our house, he would draw a preliminary plan and go over it carefully with the client, explaining how it would change life for the client and his family through what architecture could do in arranging space for convenience and beauty. Wright would be at his most enticing and eloquent, but if the client still did not like what he saw, they parted without any obligation. If the client did like the plan, he immediately paid Wright one quarter of Wright's fee of ten percent of the estimated cost of the house. This fee would include working drawings and construction supervision, plus furniture and landscape design. In a couple of years, with clients flocking to him begging for his services, Wright changed this arrangement. In our case it paid to be first. Ignorant of architectural procedures, we could not envision the many hours Wright must have spent in conceiving and developing the many building innovations brought together in our house but first sketched out in his mind. He delighted in amazing his followers by apparently "shaking a plan out of his sleeve" as he had done before the eyes of his son John before World War I with the plan for the Midway Gardens "good time place" in Chicago; and in 1935 he had astonished the Taliesin apprentices by drawing the complicated plans for the Fallingwater house while client Edgar Kaufmann was driving that morning toward Taliesin.

In his autobiography Wright said that the first showing of plans to a client was always a tense and chancy moment, but he showed no trace of nervousness as he smoothed out the large white sheet lying before us on the drafting table. "See here at the front, the only windows are in this narrow band a foot high, that runs the whole length of the living room, along the top of the wall and just under the roof," he pointed out. "People can't look in at you, and of course you can't look out. Instead, you'll be looking toward the garden side of the house, and that's all glass."

What a break with tradition! Instead of an imposing facade with elaborate entrance, just a plain exterior of wood. No elegant picture window centered in the street side of the living room. No walnut veneer table behind it, with the inevitable lamp and its large white shade, flanked by lace curtains and heavy draperies. And no sacrifice of lot space to a large front lawn. This house would be different. Instead of being designed to impress the neighbors, it would be arranged to make life pleasant, and private, for the occupants. Bad news for people who had no other source of interest than keeping track of their neighbors through furtive glances from behind the curtains.

Wright frequently described the traditional showcase effect of houses as "a Queen Anne front and a Mary Ann back." In various published works he has called this American tendency "grandomania," and it seems to be increasing. When I drive around in a new suburb I see sidewalks that are farther from the curbs, houses set farther back from the sidewalks—when there are any—and wider streets and lots. All the houses have their widest side to the street, and a lot of the money goes to make that side impressive. It all means longer utility pipe lines, fewer houses per acre, and hence much more expensive land as part of the total cost. Just cutting the grass takes a lot of someone's time.

The perspectives for "Usonia No. 1" showed a house with only a narrow band of windows under the roof on its street side, but with full-length glass doors that opened to embrace a large backyard garden. Among the innovations Wright planned were a carport, a flat roof, and a grouping of utilities and plumbing in a central stack. (Copyright©The Frank Lloyd Wright Foundation, 1954)

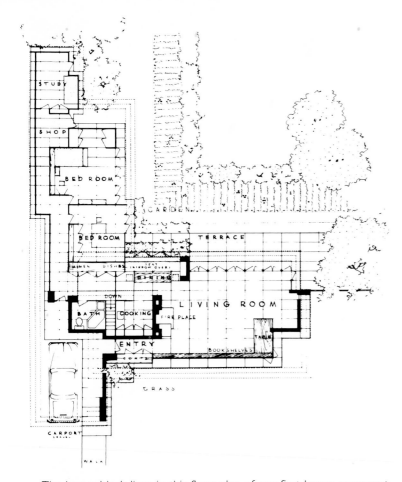

The heavy black lines in this floor plan of our first house represent the brick walls and piers which give rigidity to the lighter wooden walls. The plan is based on a two-by-four-foot module, with all window and door openings and room dimensions as multiples of these basic figures. One can see in the living room how the brick pier at the end is notched into the eight-by-four-foot table. Dotted lines of the roof indicate setbacks enabling more sun and light to enter. Terrace and living room are on the same level. Both the concrete floor and the fiberboard ceiling were scored with the module lines. (Copyright © The Frank Lloyd Wright Foundation, 1954)

Nobody has clothes lines out in back any more: the neighbors might think that you can't afford a washer-dryer. The houses are set so far back that there's no room for adequate vegetable gardens. Inside, the living rooms are so filled with expensive furniture and rugs that they are too good for daily use, and especially for children to play in. So now there are "family rooms" for ordinary living, and we are back to the Victorian idea of a parlor for guest entertaining.

But in our case visitors and guests would approach along a walkway inside the carport, and would be under shelter while waiting to be admitted, Wright pointed out. And of course the front door, in this modest house, would be plain, without the "dressing up" of a fanlight, little side windows, or expensive paneling. With a gesture toward the small basement provided (it was only eight by sixteen feet) the architect commented that a full-size basement under a house usually represents about a quarter of the construction cost, making it a very expensive place to hang laundry or store unwanted furniture. "If there's no place to store junk you'll be forced to get rid of it," said Wright, his eyes dancing.

He became positively lyrical when he talked about the interior of the house. He was already on record as asserting that the interior represents the essence of any building. "In this house," he told us, "you will have the sense of space—not space itself, but the sense of space—that most people pay ten thousand dollars for." He pointed to the bands of small windows under the roof (he called it "the system of fenestration") enabling the viewer to see the ceiling extended out beyond the walls. "These wide overhangs, going out four feet, give the feeling of shelter which is not given when there is no overhang visible from inside," he said. "The sense of shelter and the sense of space are the two major contributions of modern architecture." As a sidelight he noted that the passageway from the front door alongside the brick wall of the kitchen made it unnecessary to bring into the living room persons with only temporary business. He also called attention to the fact that the bedroom wing was completely to one side, at right angles to the living quarters, ensuring greater privacy and quiet.

While the house turned its back to the street, it opened its arms completely on the garden side. The entire wall opposite the street side was made of glassed doors running up nine feet to the ceiling. In the summer each pair of doors could stand open. With the corner windows all around, which were Wright's earlier contribution to modern architecture, the roof seemed to float above the walls, rather than pressing down on the house. (The effect of "floating" was especially notable at night from the outside, we observed after we had moved into the house.)

New ideas came at us so fast that they really did not sink in for many weeks. Just what Wright meant by making the wiring itself serve as the light fixtures was not clear until we saw it in place. Concrete floors? We had never thought about them. Wright did not talk about the concrete; he spoke of the warmth and comfort that would come by warming the floor, the absence of drafts, the elimination of ugly radiators. We saw, but did not really comprehend, a design that provided the whole outside wall of the master bedroom with glass doors from floor to ceiling. What would it be like to occupy a bedroom thus exposed? "You'll be able to look out of bed at the whole garden," Wright said with a smile. It did not occur to us until we got inside the house that something besides flowers and grass might be on the other side, looking back in.

Dazzled and enchanted by this sweeping prospect of space and privacy and a big garden, we had only one real question, asked with growing doubts: "Do you think we can still get into the new house by Christmas?" Wright did not even seem to pause to ponder the question. It was already the end of September, he pointed out. To prepare working drawings and blueprints would take weeks, and more time after that to get bids on construction. Even more important, he said, was the matter of the concrete mat, the big slab which would float on a bed of gravel. Building in the winter would be almost impossible because of the difficulty and expense of keeping the concrete from freezing, he declared. Well, there went that dream. But by that time we were so delighted by and committed to the idea of this new venture in living that we were reconciled. Besides, there was nothing we could do about it.

At least we could still write letters and memos. The first one went off just three days after we drove home from Taliesin. We had noticed that Wright had indeed reduced the house to two bedrooms, as we had suggested, but he had tacked on a small workshop with entrance off the master bedroom. It was as if I had an itch to get up at midnight or 4 a.m. and dash in there to whip a footstool, floor lamp or other bit of carpentry. I had suggested a utility room with space "for a small workbench," and Wright had seized on it as if it were my heart's desire. I wrote him on September 28, 1936:

"The more we meditated on your plans for our house, the less we want to change them, Katherine and I have decided. There is just one major change, however, which we want to make and that concerns the workshop. I am afraid I gave you an exaggerated impression of the amount of carpentering and cabinet making that I do. It really amounts to very little, and certainly not enough to justify an extra room. Instead of the workshop we would like an extra bedroom, perhaps quite a bit smaller than the others, and with its own entrance off the hall, provided you think the extra bedroom could be added for about $400 or less." That third bedroom is what brought the cost of the house up to $5,500.

The letter also invited the Wrights to dinner, along with the two apprentices who had been assigned to superintend construction, but this was ignored. I attached a memo of suggestions, such as allowing wall space for an upright piano. (We had one that had cost us twenty-five dollars, but were unaware that Wright, himself an excellent pianist, scorned anything but grand pianos.)

One suggestion did bring prompt results, but not the kind we anticipated. I wrote that we had a good mahogany table, a large round cherrywood table, two walnut dressers, and other cherished pieces. Wright stopped by our rented Madison flat unexpectedly one day (he never did announce any of his visits), took one look at our prized heirloom pieces, and said flatly, "This stuff is all prehistoric, and it will have to go." Saying which he turned on his heel and left.

Wright had complained in his autobiography that clients tended to use up all their money in building the house (perhaps he had a hand in helping them?) and then "dragged in the horrors of a bygone age" for furniture. Doubtless he saw, and seized, an opportunity in our case to prevent this with some timely action. Later, when we talked with him, he said the only proper way was to build furniture to match and fit in with the house. We promptly suggested that Katherine's cousins, Harold and Clarence Wescott,

The garden side of the house seemed to be all glass. Wright liked to say, ''Where does the house leave off and the garden begin?'' Enclosed by a thick border of shrubs, barely started in this picture, the garden was a private world for us. (Photo by Larry Cuneo)

might do the furniture for our house, since they had done some pieces for their own parents. We reminded Wright that Harold had been at Taliesin for a summer, and that he was the person who had suggested that we go to Wright. Probably sensing a way out of any furniture difficulty, Wright said they could make some designs, and send them through us to him for correction and approval.

As I look over the memos I wrote Wright in the days before we saw the floor plan I smile at the detail with which I spelled out the obvious. For instance, under "accessories" I listed water softener, water heater, and heating unit. I wanted a desk in the living room with places to file various writing projects for which there was no room at the office. In the master bedroom I specified "twin beds, cross-ventilation, plenty of closet space, full-length mirror, built-in wardrobe, space for bedding." Katherine dictated the section on the kitchen: "Built-in sink—double basin for dishwashing, space for stationary tubs here or in utility room, covered for work tables; built-in place for stove with storage space underneath; niche for refrigerator; window over sink if possible; make partition between living room and kitchen into shelves accessible from both sides, for linen, dishes and silverware. Fan to remove hot air. Concealed open door into kitchen from living room. Toe space under all cabinets. Ironing board and broom closet."

In the yard we asked for "place for hanging wash, partly enclosed yard, flower garden, vegetable garden, play area for children." Also a place for sun bathing. There was more, much more, in the memos, and all to go on a sixty-foot lot!

We were dangerously like the kind of client who cuts out a model kitchen from one magazine, a tasty living room from another, plus assorted model bedrooms and bathrooms, hands them all to an architect, and tells that harried individual, in effect, "Wrap an outside covering around these." On all this, of course, the client hangs an impossibly low price tag, and adds the injunction, "Start digging tomorrow."

Instead of flying off the handle at all the specifics which we laid out, Wright blandly ignored them and went about doing what we had asked him to do in the first place: design a five-thousand-dollar house. Meanwhile a note from secretary Gene Masselink informed me that the scale drawing of our lot was being mailed to us. He said Mr. Wright or "the boys" would be in during the next week to confer with us. "Since you are in town and can get around easier, Mr. Wright wonders if you could look up the building restrictions information and have it ready when he comes in," Masselink added.

I did not look up this information, partly because I too was busy, and mostly because I didn't even know where to look. Not that it mattered. Neither Wright nor the boys came in that week—or any of the following weeks. Maybe it was a gentle way of weaning us from the idea that Taliesin would do it all, without our lifting a finger. Eventually the contractor took care of it.

I countered Masselink's letter with one of my own, pointing out that the space in the master bedroom between wall and closets had left only six inches between the twin beds and no space on either side to make them up. Wright did not reply to this letter either, but he solved the problem in the working drawings by cutting two feet off the closet width—which still left us with ample closet space.

3.

Working Drawings
and a Double Shock

Wright was leading us, oh so gently but firmly, along the primrose path of education in house building. But toward the end of October, while we were still glowing with reflections on the drawings we had seen, we received two seismic financial shocks in delayed form.

We drove again to Taliesin for dinner on October 24, and though it was late fall we ate outside, at long tables. Seated beside us at our table was a sturdy old man with magnificent flowing white beard, introduced merely as "Uncle Enos." I learned later that he was the last survivor of the skeptical Lloyd Jones farming uncles of Wright's who inhabited the valley. All the uncles had been sure that the very next storm would topple Wright's youthful engineering marvel, the "Romeo and Juliet" windmill he had built for the aunts' school. Wright named it thus to reflect the engineering principle of a diamond integrated to a hexagon; and he made it of plain horizontal boards, to withstand wind pressure, so it was quite unlike the customary steel skeleton windmills which dotted the countryside. (Far from toppling, the windmill still stands, though now much reinforced because of age.)

We had a few moments' discussion with Wright after dinner, becoming more serious when he dropped the first bombshell, saying that we really ought to have more land than one sixty-foot lot, in order to provide a suitable setting for the house. We protested that we couldn't afford more land, but he urged us to "do something about it." Naturally I countered with my favorite weapon, another letter, which began thus:

"We argued the question of the extra lot all the way home last night, but I just don't see how we can swing it right now. The price has gone up considerably, I learned, and I am afraid its purchase would simply be too much load to carry. I will try a little later, however, to get an option on it. Probably the best thing would be to go ahead with the single lot which we now own, at least so far as plans are concerned." The statement about the price was sheer bluff on my part, as Wright probably suspected, for I had not even inquired.

And I added, referring to the "prospectus of needs" which I had handed him the night before: "I hope you understand that this is no ironclad affair which must be followed to the letter. Its chief purpose was to clarify our own ideas and to prevent overlooking any details which you might want to know about."

In the next few days it slowly dawned on us that Wright had designed the house to be exactly sixty feet wide, the full width of the lot. We suspected that even the rudimentary zoning of a suburban unincorporated area would require some sort of setbacks at the sides, and certainly the neighbors would protest. The more we thought about it the more were we certain that Wright would never consent to cut so much as an inch off the house. And of course we wouldn't have wanted him to, being already that partisan. So we talked again to the real estate agent, who turned out to be delighted to sell us more land. He suggested two lots across the street, giving us 120 feet each on two sides, since one of them was a corner lot. He took back the original lot, but the additional eight hundred dollars for the second lot wiped out almost the last of our savings, which we had been holding in reserve to cover any little extras involved in the building, not expecting that the first "extra" would demolish our cash. We did insist on a provision in the new deed that we could sell off fifty-five feet of the new property later, if we so desired. As it turned out, our desires would have had no effect. When Wright staked out the location of the house a few months later, he placed it as tightly as possible against the inside corner of the inside lot, giving the house as much "setting" as he could. Since ownership of the corner lot ran to the center of the side street, and required setbacks for road and sidewalk, any house on that fifty-five feet would have had to be no more than about fifteen feet wide.

But one unexpected result of the land switch was a much-improved orientation of the house, and a better view. Moving from the west to the east side of the street made it necessary to "flop" the floor plan, so that the main part of the house would still turn its back to the street. That wall of door-windows in the living room would now face east instead of west. Thus we would have the welcome morning sun in fall, winter and spring, pouring in to warm and cheer us, and would be spared the burning rays of afternoon entering those windows in summer. The original site, on the side of a slight rise, sloped upward toward the back, and had been completely masked ·by trees along the street. In the new location the ground sloped down from the street, and we were higher than any future houses we would be looking at from the garden side. Thus we would always have a view for miles toward the distant hills.

Did Wright quietly plan it that way, knowing that we would eventually have to switch lots? We often thought about it, but never asked. Even if we had asked, we would probably have received one of his quizzical answers, actually revealing nothing of his thoughts.

While we were busy getting the new land Wright was completing the working drawings that, we learned later, would lead to our second big shock. He wanted a formal ceremony of signing a contract and also signing the drawings, and this "double-ring" rite was duly held at Taliesin November 15, 1936, with all the formality of a small wedding, Depression-style. Technically the contract was between us and the Taliesin Fellowship, a corporation set up years earlier by wealthy friends of Wright's to free him from financial worries and the frequent legal tangles and lawsuits that grew out of the breakup of his third marriage. Katherine wrote out the contract in longhand from Wright's dictation, on a piece of newsprint paper that I fished out of my pocket. It read as follows:

Nov. 15, 1936
Contract Between Mr. and Mrs. Herbert Jacobs and the Taliesin Fellowship Architect.
The Taliesin Fellowship agrees to make the plans and let contracts and superintend a dwelling to be built at Westmorland, Madison, Wis. Said dwelling is to cost $5,500 complete according to plans and specifications identified herewith by signatures of the parties to this agreement.
A fee of $450.00 is to be included in this sum and is to be paid to the architect as follows:

25% payable when preliminary sketches are submitted and approved.
50% payable when plans are ready for letting contract.
25% payable when/as work on the dwelling progresses.
Designs for furniture and for planting will also be included in the services of the architect without additional fees.

Witnessed
Bennie Dombar
James Thomson

Frank Lloyd Wright for the
Taliesin Fellowship

Herbert A. Jacobs

Wright later told me that this was the first house he had ever designed to be built under a fixed-price contract. Young Bennie Dombar and James Thomson were two silent and rather subdued apprentices at Taliesin, and Wright said they would be superintending, and maybe helping in the construction. However he became so interested in the house that he virtually took over the supervision himself. For some of the later houses Wright charged clients a fee for the services of the superintending apprentice, and the owner was expected to furnish the apprentice with board and room.

The next thing that came along, November 30th, was an elaborate set of five pages of specifications, initialed by me and by the general contractor, P.B. Grove. Like the plans, the specifications were a new world to us, and some of the language seemed merely like longer phrases for "do a good job." They spelled out the basic simplicity and importance of the unit or module system, which was diagrammed in the drawings and would be marked by scored lines in the concrete mat and in the fiberboard ceiling of the house itself. The very first sentence of the specifications put it crisply:

"This building is to be erected upon a concrete mat laid out on a $2'0 \times 4'0$ unit system wherein the unit lines become the joint lines of the concrete and this mat must be completed before the superstructure is commenced. In the preparation of this mat the accuracy of the unit layout is most important and the joints must be made to extend two-thirds of the way through the thickness of the mat." The document specified that a strip of zinc or copper be laid in a slot cut in these unit lines where all partitions, outside

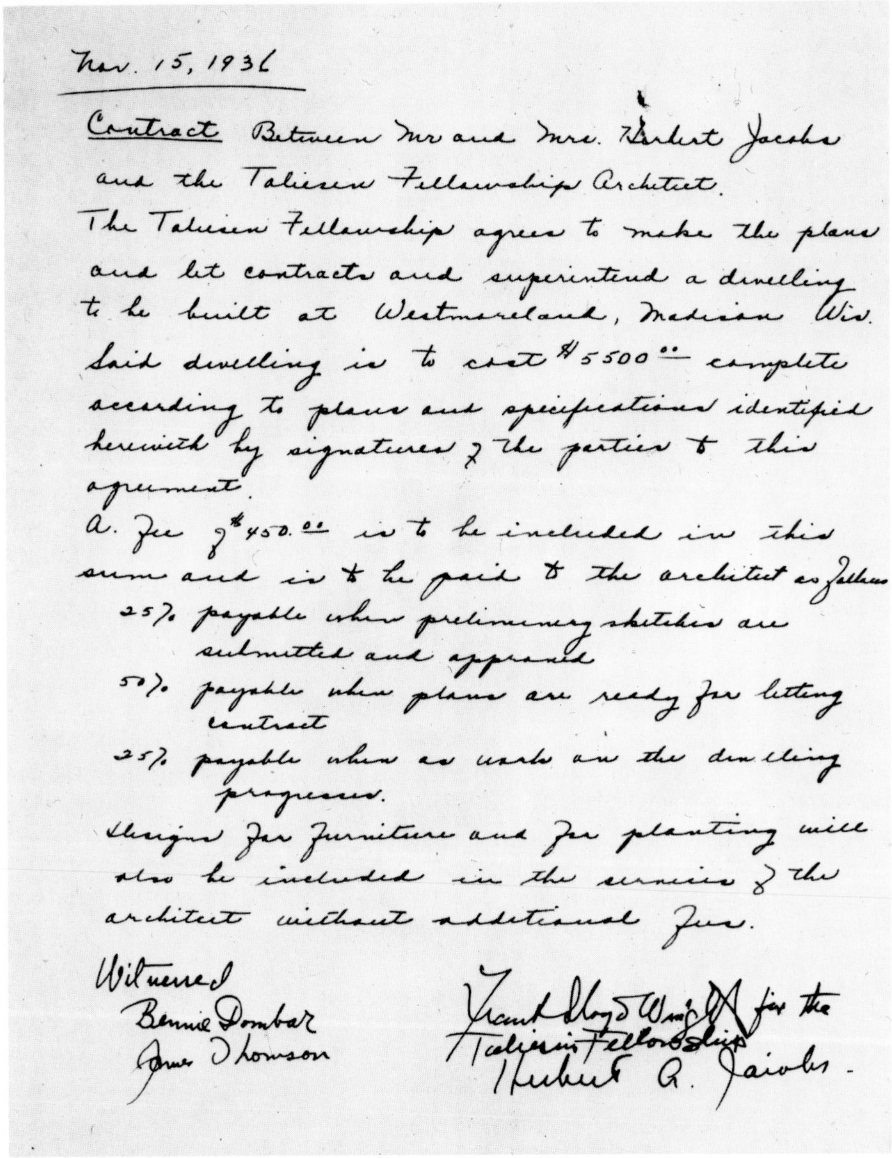

Nov. 15, 1936

Contract Between Mr and Mrs. Herbert Jacobs
and the Taliesin Fellowship Architect.
The Taliesin Fellowship agrees to make the plans
and let contracts and superintend a dwelling
to be built at Westmoreland, Madison Wis.
Said dwelling is to cost $5500.00 complete
according to plans and specifications identified
herewith by signatures of the parties to this
agreement.
A fee of $450.00 is to be included in this
sum and is to be paid to the architect as follows
   25% payable when preliminary sketches are
       submitted and approved
   50% payable when plans are ready for letting
       contract
   25% payable when as work on the dwelling
       progresses.
Designs for furniture and for planting will
also be included in the services of the
architect without additional fee.

Witnessed
Bennie Dombar
Anne Thomson

Frank Lloyd Wright for the
Taliesin Fellowship
Herbert A. Jacobs.

This contract, written on a piece of newsprint by Katherine at Wright's dictation, concerned itself chiefly with how Wright was to be paid, and specified the contract price of fifty-five hundred dollars. There was no contract for the second house.

19

walls and fenestration were to go, to serve as a weather seal. All the windows and doors followed the same unit lines, being either two or four feet, and the rafters and ceiling did likewise, so that there would be "little or no cutting" of the ceiling material, which came in four-by-eight-foot pieces.

Wright used this grid system in the dozens of houses which he later designed, modeled after the prototype established by our house. Each house was different, of course, because the scheme combined great flexibility with simplicity. He called our house "Usonia Number One" saying the word came from novelist Samuel Butler's name of Usonia for the United States, because, Wright declared, this was the kind of house that could best serve America. The word, however, does not occur in Butler's published works, I am told. It is possible that Wright saw a reference in his middle years to a small movement in America's colonial days to name this country Usona, for United States of North America, with the citizens to be called Usonians. That movement failed, along with others like it that wanted to name the new nation Columbia after Christopher Columbus, or Fredonia, to emphasize freedom. Wright's use of the word never caught on with the public, and it remained confined to architectural comments on his own houses.

There were figures, too, in the specifications, on which subcontractors could base their estimates. For the furnace, including two hundred feet of two-inch wrought iron pipe, the figure was $450. For all the hardware, $65; electric wiring and fixtures, $100. Things had to fit exactly, the specifications warned. For the brickwork, vertical joints were to be flush with the surface, set close, with mortar the same color as the bricks. The horizontal joints were to be just five-eighths of an inch high, and raked out three-quarters of an inch below the surface of the bricks. Each of the brick masses was to be just thirty-one courses high. The wooden walls, likewise, had to come out exactly as ordered. The horizontal pine boards on either side of the central core boards were unattached, and were held in place by screws in the narrow redwood battens which fitted into the boards. And the wall boards had to "come out even" at the top, ending with a batten; there could be no fudging of a slovenly top joint by the customary molding strip as a patch between wall and ceiling.

"There will be no plastering in the building. There will be no painting or staining of any kind. It is therefore important that all joints be clean and workmanship good."

We thought this and other language of the specifications rather draconic, but contractor Grove, with a wintry smile, said only, "We'll see what we can do."

And just about the time the specifications came sailing through the mail we got our second major jolt. The Federal Housing Administration, which we had been so sure would welcome this innovative, forward-looking stride into the American housing future and shelter us under its mortgage guarantee wing, gave us a flat turndown because of the flat roof. They never bothered to look at the radically new heating system, the concrete floor, the sandwich-like walls without studding, or any of the other hair curlers that Wright was proposing.

By rights we should have been disheartened, maybe we should even have given up; but like the victim of a fatal illness, we pretended that it simply didn't exist. We bounced back, full of optimism, feeling that something would turn up to save us. In fact we virtually forgot about financing until well into the following spring, on the eve of construction.

4.

Sin and Pneumonia

For a newspaperman to be scooped on his own story is not unusual, but still a sin. Like others of my craft I realized that secrets tend to leak out, and I had done my share of running around with buckets to catch and print them, but like others I was sure it couldn't happen to me. I had been working on the Madison *Capital Times* for only five months, and had been careful not to tell anyone that I thought I had money enough to build a house, let alone one designed by Frank Lloyd Wright, whose reputation had suffered because of the bills he had run up during his difficult years.

"Be sure your sins will find you out," my deeply religious mother had told me often enough. My sin, severely frowned on by editors (though they do a bit of suppressing themselves occasionally), was in withholding news I myself was involved in, and letting the opposition paper print it first.

For many months Taliesin had been furnishing a free weekly column to the *Capital Times* and its rival daily, the *Wisconsin State Journal.* Taliesin apprentices took turns composing it, and the main object was to give them practice in writing, rather than to reveal any treasures of architectural wisdom. In cold fact it was printed as a favor to Wright. One of my duties on the paper was to read copy on this and similar pieces, to make sure they conformed to the paper's style, and to keep an eye open for leads to possible news stories. By agreement, both papers always ran the column on the same day, and both set it in type a day or so ahead of use. This time the column was about our house, and Wright's notes stressing its innovative features were used.

When the column arrived in the mail, the city editor tossed the envelope to me without even a glance inside. I wrestled with my conscience—always an unequal contest—about whether to tell him it was about me and my proposed house. Cravenly, I decided to let the column appear as usual on an inside page near the back of the paper under its usual noncommittal heading, "Taliesin." But the *State Journal,* ever anxious to stick a needle into us (we tried to reciprocate), rewrote the column as a news story and splashed it on page one.

Fortunately I was out of the office when copies of the *State Journal* arrived, or the reaction of the editors might have been more brisk. In those Depression days the normal response of editors to such affronts to the paper's image was to bark, "Go down and get your pay and clear out of here!" I had seen it happen more than once. But I was out in a small town fifteen miles away, getting details on a woman who had poisoned fourteen members of her family, including eight or nine small children. Nobody had died, but that wasn't because of her lack of trying. When I telephoned the office with my story for the home edition, the city editor shouted, "You got scooped on your own story! How come?" My top-line story on the poisonings apparently warded off any more drastic response, and I was reluctantly forgiven.

But there was disquieting news almost immediately from another front. Wright's secretary Masselink wrote December 18, 1936 that the reason we had not heard from Taliesin was that Wright's "cold," which Masselink had mentioned in a telephone conversation earlier, had developed into a severe case of pneumonia. He said that Wright had passed the crisis stage, his temperature was now normal, and if no complications set in he was on the road to recovery.

A portent of the clouds of publicity that would pour torrents on us later came in a further statement that Taliesin had been flooded with mail since the news of "the $5,500 house" had been spread by a wire service story. The United Press had put the *State Journal's* story of our house on its national trunk wire.

Of course we worried about Wright, with thoughts unequally and ungratefully divided between concern for him and for our house, but his rugged frame took the pneumonia in stride, although he was then sixty-nine years old. A few months after the pneumonia we saw him on a raw spring day jump to the platform of a road grader and spin the control wheels while he waved to us to follow in our car out of a muddy Taliesin road.

Just a few weeks before the muddy road incident our winter of

Wright to Answer Need for Low Cost Housing in Madison Residence

This front-page story in the rival *Wisconsin State Journal* in effect scooped my own paper, the *Capital Times*, with the first published story about our house.

When Frank Lloyd Wright finishes building the Madison home he has designed for Herbert A. Jacobs, a Madison newspaper reporter, people are going to point to it and say:

"That's the house that very little jack built."

Wright told The State Journal today that the total cost of the house will be $5,500 including an architect's fee of $450. The small size of the fee, Wright said, makes it possible to put the house in the low cost class.

The new dwelling will represent Wright's most recent venture into the low cost housing field, long one of his major interests in architecture. It is the answer of Wright, for decades a leader in the ranks of modern architects, to the challenge of both private and public attempts to build low cost homes.

As such, it is sure to command the interest of architects throughout the country. They will be eager to see what comes from the Wright drafting tools.

Two other homes in Madison are products of Wright's creative ideas. One was built from his plans for Robert M. Lamp in 1900 at a cost of $2,000. Wright said. It is located at 22 N. Butler st. Mr. Lamp's widows now Mrs. E. S. Farness, has resided there from the time the house was built. Despite the passage of time, Wright said, this first Madison house of his is "still modern architecture."

The other was built for Prof. Eugene A. Gilmore, former dean of the University of Wisconsin law school, constructed in 1904 somewhere between $8,000 and $10,000. The Gilmores lived there until seven years ago, when they moved to Iowa City, where Gilmore became president of the University of Iowa The present occupant, who moved in when Gilmore left, is Howard F. Weiss. This Wright creation, known to Madisonians as "the aeroplane house," is at 120 Ely pl.

New Ideas Used

Jacobs recently came to Madison after several years in Milwaukee, is living at 1143 Sherman ave. with his wife and son.

Wright told The State Journal that plans for the Jacobs home had been completed and that work on the grounds was about to begin. It will be located near the municipal golf course.

The new home will contain one large living room with an extension serving as a dining, "a large and convenient kitchen, a large bathroom and three big sized bedrooms," Wright said. The house will flank a garden on two sides. An interesting feature will be the heating, which will be placed under the floors, eliminating radiators.

The architect who has been working on low cost housing plans since 1921, decided that the Jacobs home was "a preliminary study for eventual pre-fabrication." He explained that he was working toward standardized plumbing, heating, and lighting which would cost little and which could be turned out by mass production methods.

The living room will contain a large fireplace, built as "an integral structural feature made out of materials of the building itself," Wright said in a lecture at Taliesin last week.

During the lecture, in a few sentences he sketched his picture of the modern home, a home that the Jacobs' dwelling will probably typify:

"Today we have the house with big living-room spaciousness and the alcove dining room abolishing the formal dining room—the integral fireplace—the utility stack—fenestration a unit complete in itself." ("Fenestration" is the manner of arranging the windows and door openings).

"The small house is where the people live," he declared. The people, yes. But what they've got to live in now is not encouraging.

"Any cross section of the small house in America," he said, "is unfortunate evidence of grandomania," which he defined as a provincial tendency to ape the city.

Japanese 'Most Perfect'

He struck out sharply at attempts of private builders to build small houses, saying the average builder "doesn't know how to build one anymore than the average family knows how to live in one."

"And yet everyone, including big business, the magazines (and government have all taken up the small house, with the deadly inefficiencies we call 'business'—everyone, that is, except the architect himself, whose business it really is," he added.

Wright told the fellowship the Japanese house was "the most perfect thing the art of architecture has produced", saying it was to be studied, "not to copy it but to learn how a true pattern for living develops always by way of creative culture, not by borrowing patterns."

He dismissed all "housing projects to date" as attempts to "build the old home in a new way". He expressed the objective he is striving for in his plans for the Jacobs' house, declaring:

"We are again trying to build a small, compact house with a modern sense of space or the sense of space that seems to me to be modern. In this instance we are trying to build the new house in the new way that is inevitable"

AT TALIESIN

[NOTE: This series of unconnected notes was made from Mr. Wright's lecture last week to the Taliesin Fellowship on the Jacobs House to be built in Madison.]

THE small house is where the people live. "The People, Yes." But what they've got to live in now is not encouraging. Any cross section of the small house in America is unfortunate evidence of "Grandomania." Not satisfied to be simple and easy because of the provincial civilization that is ours, Grandomania is always provincial. The American village might be charming if it didn't ape the city. A milkmaid properly dressed for her work might not fail of charm whereas if she put on silk stockings, high heeled shoes and the cocked hat that belongs to the pavements she would be ridiculous. That kind of ridiculous is what I mean by "Grandomania."

The average builder of the small house doesn't know how to build one anymore than the average family knows how to live in one. And yet everyone—including big business, the magazines (and government) have all taken up the small house—with the deadly inefficiencies we call "business"—everyone, that is, except the architect himself, whose business it really is.

✧ ✧ ✧

JAPANESE SUCCESS

THE Japanese house was an ideal house for the Japanese. It is slight, low in cost; the finest example of organic architecture in the world: the most perfect thing the art of architecture has produced. I should say: one of Architecture's greatest achievements. We would do well to study Japanese domestic architecture, not to copy it but to learn how a true pattern for living develops always by way of creative culture, not by borrowing patterns.

All "housing" projects to date are "water over the dam." Nothing has really happened. "General Houses" —"Moto—Homes, etc, etc, are all attempts to build the old house in a new way. So how could anything happen? The thought in the effort is un hanged. We are looking over this Jacobs House. And here we are again trying to build a small compact house with a modern sense of space or the sense of space that seems to me modern. In this instance we are trying to build the new house in the new way that is inevitable.

Any approach to building the new house in the new way is necessarily fundamentally different. The architect must be conscious of making a pattern for good living—new perfectly suitable to living conditions in America as they are today. We are not safe in throwing away precedents (going from bad to worse) unless we have found this new pattern for living. We—the Fellowship —are endeavoring to face this reality called life out of which must come this new "pattern for living"—a term we can justly use for the organic dwelling place.

✧ ✧ ✧

HOUSES CHANGING

THE way people live in America is slowly changing with the changes in the people. The house itself is somewhat different — even now. The "parlor" for example used to be an awful thing—Wilton carpets with roses—"what-not" in one corner—marble-topped center table— machine carving—looped-up lace curtains—shades pulled down so as not to fade the roses—all of this thing that is the matter with America — whatever that is: I have just called it Grandomania. I think it is bad architecture that is the matter—really. But the kitchens were livable — then. The good life (such as it was) was lived there. Well, the parlor is gone, we've seen it go. But what most housewives have still got to have is a special "dining room." A special box, that is to say. All rooms

used to be boxes—all were boxes within one big box. Box to box. You were in a box when you were in the house and wandered from box to box. Household "regimentation" was inevitable in order to live at all in such a place.

But all this boxing, this interference with the free movements of sensible domestic life has changed: the big living room has come to stay, and there is not much sense in the separate dining room any longer. This new house we are considering has none, but the dining is amply provided for as adjunct to the big living room. Thirty-five years ago I had the idea that even the small house should have one big fireplace (the old house had no real fireplace —it had only a "mantle"—a "mantle" is furniture, not building—a piece of furniture standing up against the wall). No fireplace should be stuck up against anything—it should be an integral structural feature made out of materials of the building itself. It is becoming so. In this house it is entirely so.

Today we have the house with big living room spaciousness and the alcove dining room abolishing the formal dining room. The integral fireplace—the utility stack—fenestration a unit complete in itself.

In this newspaper column Wright set forth for the first time the principles for a new kind of American architecture which he had envisioned for our house, emphasizing space, openness of plan, grouping of utilities, and elimination of attic, large basement, and separate dining room. Such a house, he pointed out, called for a new pattern of living.

discontented waiting was much brightened by a financial rainbow reflected right out of Wright's past. Harry Haley, head of a small Madison building and loan company, telephoned me at the office to ask whether we had any arrangement to finance our Wright house. With no eye to the future, we had simply ignored the question of money after the Federal Housing Administration had turned us down. After looking at the plans, Haley called back the next day to say that his firm would be happy to lend us $4,500. Later I learned that this short, sandy-haired, very conservative man, one of four brothers in the real estate and loan business, had been born and raised in Chicago. As a young man he had often visited the great Midway Gardens, the "good time place," as Wright himself described it, for music, dining and dancing, and was enchanted by the beautiful setting Wright had created. He had seen the story on our house, and decided to take a risk where the FHA had disdained to tread.

"Uh, you know that Wright is planning an unusual system of heating through the floor," I began hesitantly. "Oh yes, we noticed that," he quickly replied, "but we figured we could put in a hot air system for about three hundred and fifty dollars if it failed." Thus, without our lifting a finger, the major problem of financing, which plagues many a home builder, was solved. (A dozen years later the Haley firm also financed our second Wright house.)

While Wright was recovering from the pneumonia effects we kept up the barrage of letters. On January 25, 1937, I wrote him:

"I enclose check for $287.50, which with the $50 handed to you Dec. 1, makes the full 75 percent of the fee, I believe. Sorry to be so late with it, but the money for the extra land had to be obtained at the same time, and this has delayed me.

"I assumed from a telephone conversation with Mr. Grove that you and he have arranged to clear up all pending questions about the house so that there may be no delay when warmer weather comes, and this is indeed very joyful news to Katherine and me."

I was assuming too much. Wright and Grove had reached no decisions, I found out many weeks later, and they did not actually come to an agreement until a heated discussion in early June,

1937. That was just before Wright left to be "honored guest" of the Soviet State and one of the speakers at an international architectural conference in Moscow. Wright seldom had a kind word for contractors, his usual attitude seeming to be that they were lucky to be allowed to work on one of his buildings, without profit, and to take a loss if necessary. Grove got the customary treatment, but his hide was tough.

I also reminded Wright that, with his approval, we had planned on Katherine's cousins to build the furniture, as they had done for their own parents. I said, cautiously, that I thought maybe we had money enough for the living room furniture at least, and it must have pleased him when I said we had started to get rid of that "prehistoric" furniture he had condemned.

"One of our great pleasures these winter nights comes as I read your Autobiography aloud to Katherine, with the inevitable discussions on architecture that follow," I concluded the letter. "But there is something missing. Where is the chapter on *our* house? You will have to write it in."

That comment may have startled Wright. The apprentices who flocked to Taliesin, and others who went there to consult him, had all been attracted to him by his lectures or by reading his book, *An Autobiography,* first published in 1932. We had done neither. We had been quite unaware of his struggles as a boy on his uncle's farm, or his brilliant years in Chicago, where he created—after apprenticeship with Louis Sullivan, "father of the skyscraper"—an American architecture of horizontal, simpler lines to replace the popular imitations of European styles. We learned of the tragic history of Taliesin, the murders of his loved ones in the arson fire of 1914, the dramatic story of the building of the "earthquake-proof" Imperial Hotel in Tokyo, the second destructive Taliesin fire in 1925, and the legal and marital tangles that preceded the very bleak years after that.

It struck us later that Wright had already lived two lives. First there was the Chicago experience of building spectacular homes for the wealthy, a life which ended in scandal when he left to spend a year in Europe with the wife of a client. Then he had a second surge of fame with the Imperial Hotel, and the experiments with concrete block houses in California, which ended in a snowstorm of legal difficulties brought on by the breakup of his third marriage, and saw Taliesin pass into the hands of strangers. His belligerent and cutting comments on his fellow architects and American architecture in general certainly kept him in the public eye, but they also scared off clients. At one point he had commented, ''There is nothing so timid as a million dollars.''

We could not of course know then that our house, along with the later Usonian houses, the Johnson administration building, and the spectacular Fallingwater house, would launch a third life, only to be cut off by World War II, when clients and many apprentices vanished. Then at the end of the war, when he was already seventy-eight years old, he would launch a brilliant fourth life, with buildings like the Guggenheim Museum in New York, the Johnson administration tower, the Marin Civic Center near San Francisco, and the daring concept of the ''Mile-High Illinois.''

5.

Construction Begins

The winter of 1936-37 carried a double chill for us. Nature produced a layer of slush that promptly froze into an icy sheet some three inches thick, which stayed on the roads for weeks, wearing into bumpy ruts. And our friends kept up a storm of horrified criticism of the floor heating of our proposed home.

"But how do you know it's going to work? This is an untried experiment," they kept repeating. Useless to point out that experiments often start out untried. This only stirred them to greater heights, ready to assault our sole defense, which was, "But Mr. Wright *said* it would work." This answer guaranteed a wave of mocking laughter. Probably that solicitous skepticism helped to toughen our hides for some of the pitfalls that lay ahead. Did it raise any inner doubts? It seems to me now, looking back, that it merely made us firmer true believers. On the other hand, I can't remember any friend saying "Great! What a thrilling experience lies ahead for you." At any rate, at least it was a topic which kept their minds diverted from other innovations, such as the "sandwich" wall construction, the flat roof, the carport, and the concrete floor. In fact I think we rather enjoyed the verbal tilts, and the feeling of being prospective martyrs.

While these critics were chirping at our future hearth we took steps which would produce the first new things about the house that we could see and touch—the furniture. I built a small model of the house out of cardboard, with detachable roof, to see how inside and outside would look. On January 31st I wrote to Harold Wescott, Katherine's Milwaukee cousin, asking him to get started on the furniture. He and his brother Clarence were devoted to racing bicycles; I wanted them to get busy with their power tools while they were still snowed in. And I had a glorious dream that the contractor would start like a fire brigade some five seconds after the frost left the ground.

Taking the table measurements off the plans, and also sending a tracing, I wrote Harold that Wright had specified a table at the end of the living room to be eight feet long and four feet wide, with the table notched to receive four inches of the adjacent protruding brick pier. When I cut out a piece of paper to scale, and tried it in the cardboard model, it looked just right, in spite of the hefty dimensions. But when the boys unexpectedly delivered the table early in the summer to our small flat, it seemed to swallow up all the space.

Adding to the congestion was the new dining table, also eight feet long, but only two feet two inches wide. "You'll be amused to know," I wrote Harold, "that just before starting this letter we examined the plans and the dimensions of the dining table and at once shrieked that it was too narrow. Then we took off a door and built a sample table the exact size of the drawing, and after putting plates and chairs along it—decided that the sage of Taliesin was right after all."

Wright had specified that he wanted to look at their designs before they started, but he made only slight changes. "Mr. Wright said that the eye should travel from the table at the end opposite the fireplace, over low hassocks, etc., to somewhat higher furniture near the fireplace, and light finally at the dining table," I wrote. "Maybe this means a couple of lounging chairs and a settee or davenport, or maybe it doesn't. Anyway, you figure it out." About the dining table I said, "I think the top slab should be of a good thickness, and the whole thing made sturdy enough so that casual guests leaning against it or sitting on it will not wreck it." For all the furniture, I reminded him that "the only general requirement I can think of is that the first consideration is for comfort, plus sturdiness."

For a contract price of three hundred dollars, including delivery—which could scarcely have left the Wescott brothers any profit—our small flat was swimming by mid-July in sturdy solid oak furniture. Besides the two big tables we got two large lounging chairs, six upholstered dining chairs that could double in living room or bedroom, a square coffee table, a hassock, and, tossed in for good luck, a child's table and two little chairs.

We cheerfully put up with the crowding, because actual construction of the house was under way at last, beginning with scraping away the sod and topsoil on June 2nd, 1937. Contractor

Grove and I had gone to Taliesin a few days earlier where he and Wright, after some occasionally heated words, had agreed on contract terms. Grove wanted the contract with me; Wright wanted it with Taliesin. The actual contract was drawn up weeks later, with me, but Wright did have the final O.K. on all bills.

Neither Katherine nor I was present for the ground-breaking. While visiting near Milwaukee Katherine had suffered a miscarriage, and was in a small-town hospital sixty miles away. I was dashing down to see her almost daily, and caring for our two-and-a-half-year-old daughter, with the help of my father. I caught a fleeting glimpse when the basement was dug and concrete poured in its forms, but immediately found myself contending with financial problems, at what should have been the most euphoric period of house building. (When the basement is dug and poured, the owner rejoices in the sight of a massive start. He faces no bills yet, no mistakes have been made—or at least discovered—and he thinks he'll be housed soon.)

Before the basement concrete had even begun to set, Grove told me the brick supplier had informed him the price would be $17.50 per thousand, instead of the twelve dollars per thousand that Wright had promised in late May for cull bricks from the Johnson administration building. The difference would be $123, Grove said, because we needed something like twenty-two thousand bricks—as many as for an ordinary brick veneer house, Wright had told me—to build the massive piers, the fireplace, and the wall around two sides of the kitchen and bathroom. Grove suggested eliminating the edging of bricks all around the concrete mat as one way to save. It looked as if we were stuck with our first "extra," but I could do nothing. Wright had gone to Moscow for the international architectural conference, and had his mind on cosmic matters.

After that brave start of the basement, activity rather subsided. Grove brought in gravel after July 1, as a bed for the concrete mat, but he spent two weeks watering it down so that it would settle completely, a good precaution. Welders came, one very plump, one rather thin, to connect up the two hundred feet of two-inch wrought iron pipe for the heating system. Wright himself, back from Russia with his mind bursting with heavy international thoughts, appeared for the day of testing the pipes at the beginning of August.

I could not sneak away from the office, but Katherine was on hand, instructed in how to operate my camera, and ready to record the historic scene of the first American floor heating project. Wright was wearing sandals and his favorite baggy pants of his own design, gathered at the ankles. Apprentices Bennie Dombar and Jim Thomson were there, along with Grove and the rotund Hugh Peake, small-town plumbing and heating contractor who seemed really interested in this new heating idea.

The only party missing was the giant national plumbing supply firm that Wright had sought to interest in this radical kind of heating, which could have meant a vast new business for them. Why did they duck? Excess of caution, probably. Their engineers had drawn up an elaborate plan, Wright explained to us earlier, involving some thirty-two valves and various controls. The only trouble was the price: $2,500. If there was to be any experimenting, I would be footing the bill, not the giant company. For this price they were willing to guarantee that if steam was introduced into the pipes, the pipes would get warm. But they refused to guarantee that either the floor or the house would get warm too. And for this noble guarantee they insisted that the local plumber assume half the risk.

"I know you people are in the business of selling valves, but I'm not buying any," Wright said scornfully when the engineers presented the plan, and with a slash of his pencil he cut out valves and controls—and any guarantee.

The representatives of the giant plumbing firm vanished, only to reappear the next winter as bewildered spectators. That left the field to Hugh Peake, though the $450 contract price was certainly not going to be any windfall. He and Grove stuffed the boiler in the basement with wood scraps, smoke from the improvised stovepipe got in everybody's eyes, and the gauge finally mounted to adequate pressure. The welded joints of pipe all held true and solid, and the pipes grew hot to the touch. So far, with no concrete mat on top, or house above the mat to warm, the noble experiment was a success. A beaming though bored-looking Wright even squatted down next to the smoking furnace to pose for one more picture for Katherine, before he and the others left with satisfied smiles.

But instead of beaming myself, I chose this moment to send the following tart letter to Wright:

Flanked by workmen and the contractor, Wright watches the testing of the floor heating system. The sandals and the baggy pants of his own design were frequently part of his costume in the summer. The three pipes at left, going to the bedroom wing, and the four at the right, circling the living room, were covered later by the concrete mat. In the left foreground are two of the L-shaped corner bricks specially designed for the house. (Photo by Katherine Jacobs)

"I heard from Grove Saturday that you have suggested battens of a contrasting wood for the house, and that this is to be an extra cost.

"In view of the 'extra' of $123 for brick, caused by a higher price per thousand than the price you quoted to Grove in May, I am not in favor of any more expense. If there are any changes, I would like them to be in the direction of cutting expense down toward the original $5,500, rather than going any higher. I simply do not have the money for such extras, however desirable they may be.

"The thing that would please me most would be speed in getting the house finished, rather than more changes which delay construction.

"I also understand from Grove that you rearranged the bathroom fixtures to preserve the triangular tub. About a month ago Grove showed me an arrangement he had planned, using a standard tub and building a towel closet at its head. As a matter of fact, Katherine and I would prefer some such arrangement, especially a towel closet and tub which permits a shower too. Neither of us is very keen on the triangular tub, but of course do not know whether this is necessary for space reasons."

I will concede now that the letter was needlessly waspish, but on the other hand, Wright had never before dealt with a client who was operating on a much-frayed financial shoestring. He replied with his usual soothing politeness.

He said that Grove was mistaken, and that there would be no extra cost for the brick, because a larger size was now planned, which would call for fewer bricks. Wright said Taliesin would pay any extra cost on the battens, and that it would be a very small item. He declared that the triangular tub would make an "admirable" shower, and suggested that we stick to Wright, rather than Grove, on details like the tub. He added darkly that if signs didn't fail, we would probably need Taliesin more than Grove later. Wright added some of the comments to the letter in his own block printing—and added an "s" to Grove's name, as he invariably did.

My recollection is that the apprentices themselves solved the matter of the bricks by producing sufficient culls (bricks with slight chips, wrong color, or radials) from the Johnson administration building job, now well under construction. The culls went for the original price quoted by Wright to Grove. The Taliesin legend later was that the apprentices, in an excess of zeal, managed to produce a whole carload of culls in just four days. For looks, Wright also insisted on specially made, L-shaped corner bricks in our house.

When Wright told us many months earlier that the walls would be "boards and battens" we had merely assumed that the battens would be like the narrow strips nailed vertically over the cracks between boards, as in Wisconsin barns. We simply weren't curious about it, and if it was explained to us that the battens were to be shaped with a tongue on the top side and a flange on the bottom to hold the shiplap boards horizontally in place, we paid no attention. Thus the sudden demand by Grove for an extra on the contract to pay for redwood battens surprised us. We didn't even know that redwood was a soft, reddish-colored wood imported from the west coast. Wright had wanted cypress for the walls, but since it was prohibitively expensive, he had settled on pine for the boards, and contrasting redwood for battens. The architect must already have been envisioning our house as the magnet it became, and wanting it to appear in its best dress.

Grove's well-meant suggestions on the bathtub were intended to save us money, as was his proposal to eliminate the edging of bricks around the mat, for he had almost no aesthetic sense. Triangular tubs were a novelty, and fairly expensive then, but Wright undoubtedly wanted one just because of the special cachet it would give, to lift the house out of the ordinary.

The affair of the battens introduced us to a characteristic of Wright that became considerably more familiar as construction proceeded: changes and refinements not only after final plans had been approved by the client, but right on through, and even after, the actual building. That restless mind of his often found ways of simplifying or of devising more dramatic architectural statements than he had originally conceived. Like an artist going back to a portrait to add a highlight to the nose that would enhance the whole center of interest, he made subtle changes, not altering the basic design, but rather "cleaning it up." Between the first set of plans for our house, and the final new set of working drawings, he had changed the size or detail of some of the minor windows. Wright often said of changes, "The best friend of the architect is the pencil in the drafting room, and the sledgehammer on the job."

In early August we left for a vacation trip to visit Katherine's family, now living on a farm in New Jersey. Such was our optimism that we expected to see most of the walls up and the roof on by the time we returned in three weeks. On our way back we ran into a special treat visiting Fallingwater, with its spectacular white concrete balconies flung out over the waterfall near Bear Run, Pennsylvania. We had heard about bristling guards and a hostile reception, but Edgar Kaufmann, the Pittsburgh department store magnate, was the soul of hospitality when we rolled up to the front door unannounced. Welcoming us as fellow clients, he showed us proudly over the whole house, where workmen were installing the huge built-in walnut veneer tables, benches and other furniture that were making the bare rooms come to life. We were very possibly the first "outsiders" to see the house.

This was the first Wright house that we had visited, aside from Taliesin, and here we could see at once what Wright meant when he talked about "the sense of space and shelter," the openness of plan where rooms and spaces seem to blend into one another. So this was the sort of thing, on a much more modest scale, of course, that we could look forward to in our own house! And our living room table, like Kaufmann's, would seem to grow from the wall. We saw for the first time huge plate glass sheets that were slotted, without framing, right into the irregular masonry walls. Kaufmann, who could afford to laugh at expense, smilingly showed us a top deck passageway where a large pane had already been broken three times by persons attempting to walk through it. As we passed the furnace room, the head of apprentice Bob Mosher rose suddenly from behind the boiler, and he said hello. He was then simply "one of the Taliesin boys" to us, here to supervise construction. Three years later he would be a dear friend, and a frequent visitor to the Usonian house.

Kaufmann insisted that we stay for lunch, and urged us to try a dip in the plunge pool near his old lodge, which he was still using while the great new house was being finished. We had never seen a plunge pool, and looked curiously at this ground-level, circular "open tank" about four feet deep and a few feet across. Kaufmann set large glasses of Scotch and water at the edge, furnished us with a couple of white terrycloth robes to wear from the inside dressing room, and explained with a smile that suits were frowned on "because we don't want any lint in the drains." We were presumably alone, and entranced by the setting of encircling conifers, the refreshing chill of the mountain stream water, and Kaufmann's two droll dachshunds yapping excitedly at us from the edge of the pool. F. Scott Fitzgerald was right about the rich being different!

We were envious of the whole delightful idea of a plunge pool, but consoled ourselves by thinking that that sort of thing was simply outside of our price range. Just eleven years later, however, we would be building our own plunge pool, with our own hands, as an integral part of our second Wright house. And it would cost a total of just ten dollars, in contrast to the hundreds which his pool had probably cost Kaufmann.

On the long drive back to Madison (the highways at that time ran right through the crowded center of every town and city, and freeways and turnpikes were still future dreams) we talked of the marvels of the Kaufmann house, its sheer beauty, the natural way in which the furniture seemed so much a part of the house, the difference that plate glass and big windows made. We were more sure than ever that we had been fortunate to pick Wright as architect.

At Christmas time Kaufmann capped his kindnesses to us by sending four heavy bronze bases for ornamental table lights. About four inches square, they had been designed by Wright with tall narrow wooden half-shades no wider than the base, which could swivel around the light socket, throwing light on wall or mirror, or on a person, as at a dressing table.

6.

"Just a Few Changes"

And was the new house, when we returned from vacation, already under roof, with swarms of workmen building walls and partitions before our very eyes? Of course not. When we dashed out to the site, what we saw seemed like a giant flat sea of gray-white concrete, with a small mound of bricks, just beginning to look like a fireplace, at its center. The edging of reddish bricks was scarcely noticeable at the borders of that vast white expanse. Rooms being framed up in a house under construction, with a clutter of bracings and piles of building materials, usually look unnaturally small. Here there was nothing to impede the eye but the distant trees and that insignificant heap of bricks.

Far from being downhearted, we were delighted to see all that concrete in place and receptively ready for walls. Grove assured us that "things would be moving right along," though he made no completion date promise. But the only workmen who appeared in the next few days were a thin, saturnine mason in mortar-whitened overalls, and a young assistant who mixed mortar and carried bricks. The mason glowered at us, never smiling all the time we knew him, but kept his spirits up with occasional nips from a pint bottle of whiskey in the back pocket of his overalls. His other habit was tobacco chewing, and he was the spittingest man we had ever seen. Occasionally he would curse Wright for insisting that the horizontal mortar joints be raked out to a precise depth, and that mortar for the narrower vertical joints be tinted to the color of the bricks. Sometimes he varied his complaints, groaning that many of the bricks were slightly curved radials (intended for the curved ends of Johnson building walls), and thus were hard to fit into our straight ones. But like many a complainer, his bark was worse than his bite, and the walls went up straight and true. When he had finished, and had washed off the white mortar stains with muriatic acid, he even grudgingly acknowledged, "Looks pretty good."

Meanwhile Wright, without saying anything to us, was meditating "just a few little changes." We had scarcely noticed the changes from the first to the second set of working drawings. They involved slight alterations, one could call them cosmetic, mainly in the window designs. On the north side of the house, for instance, where the roof was seven feet high over the long hallways to the bedrooms, Wright broke what could have been a too monotonous line of small windows at the top of the wall by replacing two stretches of windows with boards.

In later years, when many clients who were having Usonian houses built brought their house plans to us for our comments as veterans of Usonian house living, we noticed that Wright constantly made such small changes, right up to completion. Once he had established the basic placement of masonry masses and the spatial relationships of the interior as defined by walls and window-walls, these seldom changed, but the modular plan, where all openings were multiples of the basic unit, such as the two feet by four feet of our own house, made minor variations easy.

Our first confrontation came as the walls began going up. "Build the roof first, and put the house under it," Wright had suggested earlier, but Grove thought he was joking, and proceeded in the conventional way, putting up the walls first. Actually, Wright was probably thinking ahead to possible mass production of Usonian houses, where standardized walls with windows across the top of them could be more easily and cheaply built in a factory, and then lifted into place on the site, under a roof temporarily held up by tall jacks, for instance. Grove, having no such visions, decided to play it safe. In an article on our house later, Wright predicted that with mass production, houses of that type could be produced for as little as $3,500. But it was never tried.

As Wright looked thoughtfully at the plans, his eye must have rested uneasily on that back bedroom roof. Sticking out just two feet, compared to the four-foot overhang for most of the rest of the house, it looked stubby. Wright simply ordered Grove to make that small section of roof go out to four feet. Grove came to us and asked that we okay an "extra" of $35 to be added to the contract price. We said we didn't want to add another penny to

Floated on a bed of gravel, the concrete mat spreads out for living room, terrace, and bedroom wing, with the brick mass of the fireplace, and kitchen and bathroom walls, beginning to rise. The edging of bricks all around the mat barely shows here. (Photo by Herbert Jacobs)

Brickwork for one living room pier has been completed, and fireplace and kitchen walls have risen to the seven-foot bedroom roof level here. The roof and walls of the bedroom wing are taking shape. (Photo by Herbert Jacobs)

the cost, even if it would make the house more attractive looking. And that was the last we heard of it. Grove must have reported our response to Wright, but the architect never mentioned it. The roof stayed stubby.

From then on, Wright kept to the price game as faithfully as we did, but his agile mind promptly figured out ways of winning and still sticking to the price. He decided, as the brick walls of the central fireplace-kitchen-bathroom rose, that one of his favorite devices, an overhanging framework of boards, would add grace to the exterior at the bathroom end of the brick mass. Wright used such structures frequently over patios and entrance ways, obtaining the play of light and shadow that he always sought. Both bathroom and kitchen walls were climbing rapidly under the ministry of the expectorating mason, so Wright had to move fast. He wanted the overhang, plus an added effect to be obtained by lowering the height of the bathroom walls by a couple of feet.

Grove protested, but Wright argued that Grove would save enough, by eliminating two feet of brickwork and the cost of laying it, to pay for the wooden framework, and Grove finally agreed. He was neither for nor against aesthetics; he just didn't care about that sort of thing. But after the framework was in place he conceded that it did indeed improve the look of the house from the street. Wright had lost at the rear of the house, but he won at the front, where it was much more visible, and had kept to the contract price.

Grove was also having trouble with the walls. Wright had specified the cheapest pine boards for the vertical core boards forming the center of the sandwich walls. In later Usonian houses he used somewhat more expensive coarse plywood for the core, and construction was easier, but with our house cost was the determining factor. The core boards kept falling down, and the carpenters had to brace them with temporary strips near the top, and anchor the side braces with weights, because it was impossible to nail into the concrete mat. The bedroom wing, with a height of only seven feet, was somewhat easier than the living room wall, at nine feet. All the core boards had slots the width of the board, to receive a three-inch fin binding them to the mat.

I was then a purist, and something of a blind devotee of Wright, with unfortunate results in one instance. Grove said to me, when his minions were starting construction of the casement

Core boards are in place here for the bedroom wing, ready for the horizontal boards and battens to be screwed to both sides. The mullions were plain two-by-fours, rabbeted out as for a doorjamb to receive the framed glass doors. The rafters, each made of three two-by-fours one atop the other, were given a slight crown with wedges between them, making the roof shed water more easily and representing a construction economy. (Photo by Herbert Jacobs)

windows over the dining alcove, "There doesn't seem to be any support, above or below, for those window mullions."

"Just follow the plans!" I said impatiently. "Wright certainly knows what he is doing."

"Well, if you want it that way, that's the way I'll do it, but I still can't see what's going to hold those windows up," Grove muttered.

I did not even think it important enough to call to Wright's attention. But Grove was right. Somewhere along the line, in preparing the second set of plans, there had been a slip-up. To make a wider shelf above and behind the bench on the wall side of the dining table, and provide an interesting break in the appearance of the house from the garden side, Wright had moved the line of windows out from the supporting wall to the edge of

The nine-foot living room glass doors and the casement windows above the dining table are in the process of being installed, and exterior boards and battens are already in place. (Photo by George Kastner, courtesy of Brian Spencer)

The three layers of two-by-fours for the roof are shown here before being sheathed by fiberboard on the underside. At lower left are windows in the corners of the bedroom wing hallway which stood open in summer for ventilation. The device on the rafters is a telephone connection. (Photo by George Kastner, courtesy of Brian Spencer)

the roof. Without the bearing of the wall, and with insufficient help from the rafters, in a little over a year those windows began to sag. I wedged a couple of two-by-fours under them for temporary support, making them intentionally ugly and precarious-looking. And I called them to the attention of one or more of the Taliesin apprentices who stopped to view the house as part of their architectural education. The word got back rapidly to Wright, and he sent in an apprentice who rapidly built two small brick piers to carry the load, and also support a large flower box. In my view the end result was more attractive than it had been when first constructed.

Word of this strange new dwelling spread fast when the roof and walls made it highly visible, and so the visitors began—a stream that never dried up all the time we occupied the house. When we dropped by late in the afternoon we would find as many as a dozen persons wandering around, gaping, measuring, bothering the workmen with questions. Since the construction jobs were all subcontracted, we didn't worry about paying for any time spent in answering questions, and the workmen, on their part, soon learned to answer questions on the run, with a noncommittal "don't know."

At first the carpenters were skeptical about those sandwich

walls, but later, when some of the walls were completed inside and out, they liked to show off how solid they were by striking them approvingly with their fists. The relationship of the battens to the wide pine boards seemed to puzzle visitors the most. The battens had a tongue on the top, to fit into the groove on the bottom side of the shiplap boards, and a flange on the lower side of the batten to go over the upper, sloped-back edge of the pine boards, making a watershed for the outside walls. Screws through the battens to the core boards held the pine boards in place, and permitted some play to accommodate temperature changes. Visitors were constantly carrying scraps of the lumber to the carpenters and asking, "Just how do these go together?" The carpenters had a template, or model, a foot wide and the exact height of the wall, made of scraps of boards and battens spaced evenly. They measured frequently as the walls went up, to make sure that all the boards were

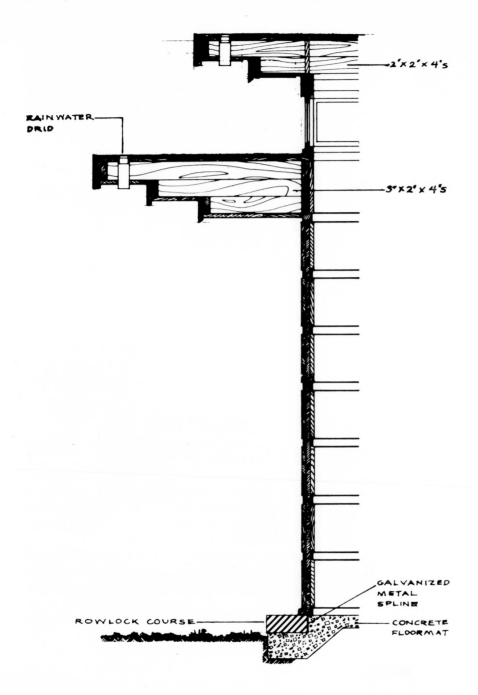

RAIN WATER DRID

2" x 2" x 4's

3" x 2" x 4's

GALVANIZED METAL SPLINE

ROWLOCK COURSE

CONCRETE FLOORMAT

Principles of the solid "sandwich wall" construction, which our house was the first to have, are illustrated in this cross section of a typical Usonian house wall. Battens—screwed to the middle core boards, tongue-and-grooved for the upper wide boards, and with a shiplap to hold the lower board and shed rain—kept the wide boards in place. Vapor-lock building paper was placed on both sides of the core boards. The lower rafter courses were stepped back to let in more sun and light. A galvanized metal spline or fin sealed boards to mat. Refinements made after our house are shown in this drawing, including smaller sizes on some rafter courses, use of plywood to replace the cheaper core boards, and deepening of the rim of the mat. (Copyright 1976 by John Sergeant, reprinted by permission of Mr. Sergeant. First published in *Frank Lloyd Wright's Usonian Houses,* © 1976 Whitney Library of Design) spaced alike, and so that there would be no ripping of a board at the top. The top of each wall had to end with the near-width of a batten.

Like conspirators, or children playing a game, we pretended that we too were just visitors, which not only saved us from being besieged by questions, but also gave us a chance to pick up scathing or bewildered comments. A few individuals were plainly hostile, but most were friendly, eager to learn something new. For some reason we did not fear vandalism or petty theft, and in fact there was none. Throughout the building period we remained spectators, rather than participants.

The story of one brusque encounter was retailed to us by contractor Grove with much relish, after Wright had paid a surprise visit to the site. He arrived just as a young and rather self-assertive Madison architect, who had designed several local houses in the stark and austere International Style, had brought Walter Gropius, the high priest of Germany's Bauhaus School of modernist architecture, to look at what Wright had been up to. Protocol required at least a telephone call to Wright to ask whether he would mind having Gropius see the house, but the Madison architect had not done this.

Red-faced at Wright's arriving so inopportunely, he introduced Wright and Gropius, and then suggested that Wright might like to show Gropius through the building and explain the construction. Wright loathed the International Style, considering it an unintelligent, misconceived imitation of his own organic architecture. Scornfully Wright turned away and refused to have anything to do with Gropius. As he left, he snorted to the Madison architect, "Why don't *you* talk to him? He'll understand *you*."

The double affront to his pride—what Wright saw as a breach of etiquette in the failure to ask permission to visit the house under construction, and then the request that he act as guide to an advocate of a kind of architecture he not only detested but considered an uncomprehending plagiarism of his own style—was too much for Wright's usual urbanity.

A few weeks later, though, Wright was in a cheerful and expansive mood as he arranged the photographing of the house for *Architectural Forum*. The magazine, then a division of Time-Life-Fortune, was devoting its entire issue of January, 1938, to Wright, a signal honor considering that he had spent so much of his time attacking traditionalists in architecture. Besides the Jacobs Usonian house, the issue would celebrate Kaufmann's house Fallingwater, and the just-completed Paul Hanna house in Palo Alto, California, where Wright used a honeycomb hexagon as module. Construction pictures of the Johnson administration building, and of what Wright playfully called a "cottage" for Herbert Johnson (it cost some $250,000) would also be included. Wright had good reason to look forward to a new burst of architectural activity at the age of seventy.

For the benefit of the photographers, the framed glass windows and doors for our house seemed in place, but most were merely tacked in with cleats, rather than hinged. To give the house the appearance of being lived in, some of the windows and doors were lightly nailed into open positions for the mid-November pictures.

The close relationship of house and garden, and of part of the house to the rest, show in this picture. It was taken from the far end of the bedroom wing, looking toward the living room. (Photo by Herbert Jacobs)

Doors and windows are wide open here to catch the summer breezes, and the garden is in full production. The corner doors closed against each other, eliminating the need for a corner post. The Aeroshade roll screens could be lowered to any level. (Photo by Pedro Guerrero)

This five-page, day-to-day record of the first stages of construction of the Usonian house came to light by accident a few days after the manuscript of this book went to the typsetter. I had forgotten that I wrote it, and discovered it in the midst of several blank pages while I was idly thumbing through an old diary.

New House in Westmorland, Madison.
Frank Lloyd Wright, architect.

At the suggestion of Harold Wescott, Katherine and I went to Taliesin to see Mr. Wright early in August, 1936. He thought a house such as we wanted could be built for $5,000. "Are you sure you want a $5,000 house?" he said. "Most people want a $10,000 house for $5,000."

A schedule of requirements was submitted to Mr. Wright Aug. 24, and he called it "very sensible."

On Oct. 1 preliminary sketches were furnished by the architect. On Dec. 1 the completed plans were signed by architect and owner, dated as of Nov. 15.

In December the Westmorland Realty Co. refused to permit a house 60 feet wide on Lot 2, Block 10, which had been purchased in August.

New land was sought, and late in December lots 7 and 8, block 3, across the street from the original lot, were secured.

Late in May, 1937, Mr. Wright set the elevation of the house, by telling a workman when to stop driving a stake.

June 1-3, two farmers and a team scraped off the surface dirt and sod.

June 7-16, Two laborers dug the basement and a trench bringing in city water.

June 16, carpenters laid forms for the walls of the basement.

June 17, the basement walls were poured, + the next day the top outside forms were taken off.

June 18, all forms were removed.

June 21 digging of septic tank and dry-well was begun, and completed in 10 days.

July 12 workmen started leveling dirt, and the basement floor was poured.

July 22 - furnace installed.

July 25 - heating pipes began to be laid - (plumber, welder and helper)

July 29 - welding and leveling of pipes completed, and Pipes tested with 60 pounds water pressure the day before.

Aug. 3 - (Great day) Mr. Wright and Grove superintended a test of the heating system, using wood on temporary grates of piping to fire the boiler. Got up steam of 5 pounds. Sand near pipes heated quickly as far as four or inches away, though the pipes were uncovered. Expansion was about one inch. Wright expressed great pleasure with the way this job was done. He boasted that with this system we would be able to open all the doors in winter.

Aug. 9 - Bricklayer runs up white brick wall in basement, pour concrete for hearth. Puts in oil tank, pour concrete over pipe sleeves.

Aug. 10 - 4 courses of brick for chimney, and hearth laid. Rough floors for kitchen and bathroom. "Young feller, you'll be a lot older when that ash pit is filled up."

Aug. 10 - Chimney run up to five feet.

Aug. 12 - Discover east end of fill and pipes have sunk 6 inches.

Little done in next few days.

Aug. 18 - Kath and I go to Taliesin to demand more cooperation with builder.

Aug. 20 - Start pouring walls; finish in 5 days.

Aug 26 - Sept. 7 - nothing done.

Sept. 8 - Tear down red bricks of chimney. Begin Jay
4 courses for lining & recess stack.

Sept. 9 - Jay fireplace on new design.

Sept. 9 - Relay back of fireplace.

Sept 14-17 Run kitchen bathroom, carport, up to 7 feet.

Sept 20-21 - place metal strips in floor to hold walls.

Sept 21 - "Don't run up that north wall." Jim Thompson tells Earl (Wood) today, until I see

Changes made in final plans of house, (done in April, but not shown to clients.)

The front door was recessed 2 feet, windows were removed above entry coat closet, living room was widened 2 feet to width of 18 feet, all flower boxes were eliminated, windows over dining seats were pushed out one foot, six windows instead of five & were placed in master bedroom cutting closet space to four feet on each side of room, doorway into back hall was widened from 2 to 4 feet, east window was removed from back bedroom, closets were shifted in Susan's room.

you tomorrow, we may want to change the height." Learned today that door in jog of north wall has been eliminated.

Foster has waited two days for power connection, which was paid for 3 weeks ago.

7.

"Let's Start Living In It"

The amused carpenters told us about the photographic binge and sudden flowering of open windows. We had already begun to wonder how much longer we would have to wait. A chance remark of contractor Grove triggered action. He said that the carpenters had rushed to enclose the house before the cold and snow arrived, but would probably take their time "for most of the winter" with the interior boards and finishing. We could picture them, snugly warm while burning *our* oil, dawdling over a few boards and cupboard doors, and probably working some days on their own and other houses. Why not start living in the house as soon as possible, we said to ourselves.

I told a sort of dingy gray lie to Grove, saying the bank was demanding that we move out of our rented flat because they had another tenant clamoring to get in. Grove may not have believed me, but he agreed to try to speed things up so that we could be in the house by the end of November. He pointed to some inconveniences: the carpenters would still be around, piles of lumber would fill much of the living room floor, some gaping holes would have to be plugged, but we could be in well before Christmas!

Although Grove warned that "the house isn't even wired yet," that task took scarcely two days. After all, the budget allowed only a hundred dollars for both wiring and fixtures. We could see why when the carpenters and an electrician rapidly hung a plain piece of channel iron on brackets from the ceiling. It was three inches wide across the bottom, an inch deep, and open at the top. The insulated wires lay inside, connected to light bulb sockets which half-spiraled round it at two-foot intervals along the sides and bottom. Another channel iron, at right angles, ran down the ceiling of the two nearest bedrooms. (In a more expensive house the lights would have been concealed in a cove.) Far from being

impressed by this economical lighting system, one workman, possibly raised amid dime store lamp shades, sneered for our benefit: "First the house looked like a barn; now it looks like a sheep shed."

Just before we moved in, we were faced with our first "extra" in the furnishing of the house, in addition to the furniture already produced by the Wescott cousins. With all that glass—five times the amount in the conventional house, Wright had said—we would need some sort of shades or screens. Wright was ready for that one too. He had told the salesman for the Waukesha Aeroshade Company, a Wisconsin firm, to call on us. Instead of curtains or draperies we would have roll screens, fastened at ceiling height. Sitting in the salesman's car late one afternoon, after he had measured the space, I argued with him over price. He wanted to sell me their deluxe brand—half-inch basswood splints tapered top and bottom to overlap, so that air could blow through, but they would be impervious to the viewer from outside. I insisted on the cheaper style, with a slight space between the splints, and no bevel. The salesman objected that these might prove embarrassing in the bedrooms, because a viewer would be able to distinguish shapes in a lighted room, but I brushed this aside, determined to stick to economy. However, when the screens were installed a few days after we moved in, they were the beveled, deluxe variety. The salesman was apologetic but proud. He said he was giving them to us at the price of the cheaper ones because "these are what you really ought to have for this house, and we figure the advertising will be worth it to the company." This was another portent of the hordes of the curious who would be heading our way, but of course we did not realize it, and were merely grateful.

The move into the house took place on Saturday, November 27, 1937, a warm and sunny day, and we had so few goods that a small van handled everything with one trip. The only minor mishap occurred when a mover tripped and fell over a stack of lumber while he and I were carrying my old oak desk to the back hall. He wasn't hurt, though, and nothing could hurt the old desk, which I had had since high school days. (The built-in desk which I had suggested to Wright could go at the south end of the living room, for papers and writing at home, never did materialize. For a few months my old desk stayed in the back hall, where I later built a workbench. By that time the penny-pinching publisher for whom I worked had decided to buy new desks for the news staff—and having discovered that children's desks were cheaper, he bought those. When I found that I could get only one knee under my new desk, and had to sit sideways to type, I brought my old desk to the office.)

We shared the living room with a long stack of boards and battens four feet high, and a pile of plywood slabs which would soon become doors for hallway and bedroom closets and kitchen cabinets. Outside the glass door of the living room a big power saw stood, swathed in canvas against possible rain or snow. To this day the delicious smell of fresh-sawed lumber brings back happy memories. At the time that odor helped to make us feel that we were part of the building experience at last.

The next day, Sunday, remained sunny, but the thermometer had suddenly dropped to ten above zero, and a strong wind whistled around the corners and under the roof overhangs. We basked in the warmth of the sun's rays through the garden-side glass wall of the living room, and went around feeling the floor repeatedly, scarcely able to believe that it was actually heating the house. Our old gas stove had fitted into the kitchen slot assigned to it, and was connected. Katherine decided against filling the kitchen shelves with foodstuffs and dishes brought from the rented flat until the cupboards achieved doors.

But the house did seem unusually breezy, which we had not noticed the night before because of the mild weather. Some amateur detective work led to the slot windows between the brick piers at the south end of the living room. But there weren't any windows! Just a board laid against the opening, which let the wind come rushing in on either side. Fortunately we had pillows, and enough rags to stuff the rest of the openings, and the house became nearly draft-free. Small air leaks appeared in other places, but they gradually disappeared over the next days and weeks as the carpenters continued to finish their work.

The activity in sealing up the slot windows marked our transition from spectators, watching somebody else build the house, into active participants in finishing and in perpetually changing the house. I suspect that few houses remain static, and certainly Wright houses seem to lend themselves easily, one might say willingly, to constant modification and adaptation. Wright himself was always changing Taliesin, tearing out partitions or windows, and altering spaces, partly to give the apprentices practice in building, but mostly because his mind was never satisfied. He seldom altered the basic plan, but found plenty of scope in changing details. To the vast irritation of the apprentices, Wright seemed mostly to decide to carry out such changes just as they were straining their energies to bring off one of the big parties for guests and clients that were a feature of Taliesin life. We witnessed one such hurry-up job when we arrived early for a musical evening in the Taliesin theater. Wright was directing a crew of apprentices in laying a new floor in the orchestra space, because a visiting musician wanted the grand piano to be on the same level as the other instruments. "If that's the way he wants it, that's the way he's going to have it," Wright said briskly. The last board was nailed down and the floor hastily swept with scarcely time for the apprentices to switch from work garments to their dress-up clothes as musicians.

It took us a while to learn the lesson, but we repeatedly encountered examples of how Wright's plans simply had to be carried through to the last detail in order to achieve the results he had sought. Bookshelves in both our Wright houses illustrate what I mean. When we moved into the Usonian house we were impressed by the shelving, which marched along the entire street side of the living room wall. Counting up our own books, we had asked for about twenty-five feet of shelves. Wright provided us with four times that amount, explaining that the shelves were needed to make the wall rigid. We noted with pleasure that the shelves did not begin until four feet from the floor. No more squinting at titles below the knees! While the shelves looked great to us just as they were, in a few days the carpenters added continuous redwood strips, an inch and a half wide, along the front of each shelf, and they suddenly came alive and stood out as an architectural feature in their own right, rather than just something utilitarian. The same minor miracle involving bookshelves was repeated in our second house. The plans called for one long shelf the sixty-foot length of the living room back wall, but I didn't think it was really necessary. Once again, before our eyes, when the shelf was prop-

As Wright intended, the great mass of the fireplace dominated this end of the living room. The car under the carport overhang can be seen peeking past the front door. Along the ceiling at upper right the simple channel iron lighting fixture shows above a corner of the dining table and the doors of the hallway storage closets. The furniture, except for the child's rocker, was made from plans approved by Wright. (Photo by Herbert Jacobs)

erly installed with a fascia trim, it "pulled the room together" and provided the necessary architectural transition between mezzanine ceiling, masonry wall, and floor.

We were fortunate that the three men who held the carpentry subcontract in the first house—two brothers named Loder, and their father—held to the old German tradition of careful, accurate work. Soon they had the slot window between the brick masses at the south end of the living room filled with small squares of plate glass with redwood pieces between them. Well before Henry Moore began cutting holes in his sculptures, Wright was breaking up his masonry masses with vertical cuts to let in light and shadow. The slot windows made an interesting transition from the horizontal lines of the board and batten walls to the vertical forcefulness of the nine-foot glass doors into which they so subtly introduced the viewer.

We got a strong reminder of the need for shades that first week, when I spent the morning of my day away from the office unpacking and putting things away. After lunch, exhausted, we dropped onto our twin beds for a rest, but we soon heard voices and a sort of mechanical rapping on the outside walls of the hallway. In a moment three shambling elderly men appeared, walking in front of our windows, but scarcely glancing inside. They were the township board of supervisors having a quick look at the newest dwelling in the area after their monthly meeting. They had simply walked around the house, absent-mindedly rapping the walls with their knuckles, and voicing the usual banalities as they moved along. "Strange, all right," we heard one say. "Yeah, different," said another, as they passed out of earshot.

Little did they know, these plodding truck farmers, that they were nurturing a viper in their midst. Within a year I would be one of a handful of agitators leading "the plats"—the unincorporated subdivisions of the township that encircled much of the city—in a successful rebellion to wrest the town government from their rural control and replace them with a slate of commuting suburbanites. (Parenthetically, our victorious group was little better at governing, the chief difference being that we replaced the more spec-

Doors of the two closets in the master bedroom had hanging space behind one and fixed shelves behind the other. I made the twin beds and Katherine made the monogrammed muslin bedspreads. (Photo by Herbert Jacobs)

The five door-windows of the master bedroom went from floor to ceiling. The open closet door shows the fixed shelves with their fascia edge. The chair is one of six that were scattered through the house except when used for extra seating at the table. (Photo by Herbert Jacobs)

The dining alcove appears beyond the fireplace. A portion of the seven-foot bedroom roof—carried in over the closets and dining table—shows here, giving the two-level effect which Wright often sought in ceilings. The photographer has grouped the living room furniture close to the fireplace. (Photo by Pedro F. Guerrero)

tacular fist fights and bloody noses of the old board with verbal pyrotechnics and pieties about good government.)

We rejoiced when the Aeroshades were installed by the end of the first week, because it would no longer seem necessary to undress in the dark, but what struck us most forcefully was the different aspect at night when the shades were lowered. In both living room and bedroom we suddenly became enclosed, the mauve tone of the shades making a glowing wall that reflected light in contrast with the daytime feeling of almost being a part of the outdoors. The novelty was such that we promptly went outside to see how the whole side of the house glowed evenly, with the roof seeming to float above it because of the reflection through the high fenestration on the street side, and from the shades on the garden side.

The fireplace was another novel pleasure, since neither of us had ever lived, except for short visits, where there was such an amenity. This fireplace had the added charm of a hob at one side of the opening, a delightful warm place to sit and toast, watch the flames, and now and then rearrange the logs for better burning. Outside and inside, the house had a litter of scraps of wood, and we were so enthusiastic, burning them each night, that the sudden intense heat cracked the rear wall bricks of the fireplace. It did not occur to us that these were regular bricks, like those in the piers and walls, rather than firebrick. After many a fire, with oak chunks succeeding pine scraps, and with the fire eating dangerously close to the kitchen on the other side, a Taliesin apprentice replaced the bricks with firebrick, on condition that we immediately blacken them with a fire, so that Wright would not notice the difference. The apprentice said that Wright had a prejudice at that time against firebrick.

I put in a mailbox which joined those of half a dozen other residents along the street on a rack two blocks away. At Christmas time the mailman delivered there, unknown to us, one of Wright's choice Hiroshigi prints from his vast collection of

The brick piers at the south end of the living room show here, along with the slot window which provided an architectural transition from the horizontal pattern of the wall boards and battens to the verticals of the bank of door-windows. On the wall is a Hiroshigi print from Wright, and on the table the iron bowl from the Johnson house. At the right end of the big table stands the floor lamp which I made from lumber scraps. The board and batten paneling of the ceiling was put up shortly before the picture was taken. At the extreme right, the pattern of "raked joints" of the bricks at the end of the fireplace can be seen. (Photo by Pedro F. Guerrero)

Japanese prints. I say unknown to us, because it fell off the mailbox, being too big to go into it, and got buried in the snow for four days before we found it.

To guide delivery men, instead of being forced to say "Uh, we're in that unusual house with the flat roof," I cut the street number out of a piece of pine with a scroll saw, and wedged it into the mortar joint of the carport pier. It was still there when I passed the house forty years later.

The hallway next to the dining alcove, leading toward the bedroom wing, took on more character when the carpentering Loders hung the two-foot-wide plywood doors on the twelve feet of closet space. Shelves two feet deep easily held all our dishes, linen and bedding. Two of the doors ungratefully warped immediately, and Grove forced the supplier to replace them. The room doors, on bedrooms and bathroom, were a lightweight thin veneer, with a waffle grid core. Bennie Dombar and Jim Thomson, the two Taliesin apprentices theoretically in charge of construction of the house, made elegant trays out of sawed-off portions of these doors, and presented them to us for Christmas.

We made the last closet in the row leading to the bedroom hallway into a telephone booth, two feet square, which proved a convenient soundproof communications center when little pitchers began to develop big ears and curiosity. Once, when Wright was there for dinner, a long distance call came for him. He was sitting comfortably in front of the fireplace, and to my astonishment refused to get up. "Just tell them I don't care to come to the phone," he told me. This made difficulties with the operator, but she finally gave up trying. At the time it seemed incomprehensible to me that anyone could refuse a long distance call—as if to do so would violate some federal law—but Wright made his own laws.

46

Twenty years later, I was in his studio office at Taliesin the day of his eighty-eighth birthday, when a television reporter called from Madison to ask for his birthday views on the world. "If it isn't worth your while to come out here, it isn't worth mine to talk to you," Wright snapped, and hung up. This from a man who loved publicity, and had even become something of a television personality in his eighties.

A few days after Christmas the Loder brothers discovered that their carpenter contract money had just about run out, and there wouldn't be any more. Suddenly, the nails and boards flew. They still worked carefully and well, but they moved a lot faster. In just a few days the house was complete, and all ours.

One shocking surprise came just after we had moved in. Either Grove or one of the carpenters remarked, in the deceptively casual tone of such persons, "There don't seem to be any screens provided for this house." A quick check of the plans showed that he was right. By that time architect Wright had gone to New York and would proceed from there to the Taliesin winter quarters in Arizona. I wrote, full of indignation. Anyone who has lived through a Wisconsin summer knows that flies and mosquitoes are always ready and eager to join the family, along with kamikaze bombardments of June bugs on a hot summer's night, occasional swarms of May flies, and inquisitive wasps and bees.

Wright replied in January, 1938 from Phoenix that he was sure he had drawn plans for screens; but no such plans could be found. Since I still owed $125 on his architectural fee, representing the twenty-five percent specified for supervision of construction, I wrote that I planned to use this money for screens. He promised to send plans; by April one of the apprentices produced them, and Grove had the screens made and installed.

8.

To Live
Inside a Picture

"You're going to be living right inside a beautiful picture," an artist friend told us when he first looked at the plans and the cardboard model I made of our house. (I believe he was commenting on his vision derived from the plans, rather than my craftsmanship on the model.) Keeping his thoughts carefully compartmented, he deplored Wright's boast of "honest arrogance" and his frequent attacks on fellow architects and their works, but nevertheless highly admired Wright the architectural innovator and genius. We recalled his words, now that the house was ours alone (except, of course, for those ceaselessly circling cars of the curious). Beauty is often in the beholder's eye, and we were willing to take his word. But would we also find the house pleasant, convenient and comfortable?

We seemed scarcely settled down in the house when we went out to speak about it—as did Wright. He and Katherine spoke to two different Madison women's groups, and sex discrimination was rampant as usual in those days: Wright got $10, and she got thanks. On paper I came out ahead, because I got $15 for a talk to a Milwaukee suburban housewives' club, with lunch thrown in, but got no travel cost.

Katherine wrote out her speech before giving it, and I will quote and condense much of it, because the talk gives an excellent picture of the house as we were experiencing it then. Also it represents one of the all-too-few opportunities for women to speak formally about the houses they live in. So many persons had already appeared at our doors that Katherine knew what would interest most of her listeners about the house.

She began with something of a shocker, saying, "I am convinced that the housewife's opinion cannot be regarded except as

to a few basic needs of her family, if the architect is to have complete continuity of design throughout."

The Taliesin apprentices were already learning the importance of good kitchen design (Wright often labelled the area as "workspace" rather than kitchen in his drawings), taking turns at cooking, and practicing the arts of serving meals and creating attractive table settings. Katherine stressed the practicality of our own kitchen, despite its small size of seven by eight feet, in contrast to the large kitchens of houses of that era. The floor space, in fact, was just four by five feet, and the room itself, hidden from the living room behind the fireplace stack, was an inside room lighted by clerestory windows from above, and open to the dining space opposite.

One of the frequent comments about the kitchen as an inside room had been "I don't think I'd like that," but Katherine told her audience: "The dining room alcove faces the east, with windows to the ceiling, starting four feet from the floor. Instead of one small window over the sink I enjoy this lovely view over the hills through the big windows. None of the exterior wall space of the house is sacrificed for the kitchen, but I have the pleasure of the best view while I work."

Katherine had an answer too for those accustomed to a separate dining room and a kitchen with a door to close. "Your guests can look right into the kitchen," had been the criticism. She pointed out that the kitchen was partly screened on one side by open shelves carrying bright objects like a tea cozy, cookie jars and trays, which hid the stove, while a refrigerator behind a partition on the other side of the opening concealed the sink. The open shelves on the dining side rose to join a whole array of open shelves which covered the back wall of the fireplace, with runners of ivy cascading down, a collection of Mexican plates with jolly colors and figures, and old coffee cans—painted Wright's favorite Cherokee red—holding dry cereals and other kitchen needs. And guests could look not only at the pine and redwood shelves, but also at a back wall of brick, and the natural wood of cupboard doors. Below the cupboards was eight feet of counter space. "Granted, this kind of arrangement does not become a formal life," Katherine said, "but please remember that it was designed for a woman who does her own work, and who prefers the simple and informal life. Most of us who have a fifty-five hundred dollar

Trays, a cookie jar, and an elaborate European tea cozy decorate the open shelves which screen the stove. Above are coffee cans painted Wright's favorite Cherokee red, for cereals. (Photo by Herbert Jacobs)

The high-ceilinged kitchen, extending two feet above the main roof, is seen here from across the dining table, with Katherine standing at the counter. The open shelves at the left are at the back of the fireplace, and those in the foreground hide the stove. (Photo by Herbert Jacobs)

house do live a simple life." She proved later that the kitchen was big enough to allow preparation of buffet meals for forty to fifty guests.

She might have added that this open-style kitchen enabled her to remain in close touch with her guests when she had to be in the kitchen during the various stages of the meal. And the central location of the kitchen, as she discovered later with more children, was an excellent command post from which to keep an eye on them in garden, terrace, living room, or bedroom wing.

Because the kitchen ceiling extended three feet higher than the main roof, and had a clerestory window in it which could be opened, most cooking odors were simply wafted upward, though Katherine conceded that if you liked corned beef and cabbage or similar hearty dishes, you could expect the odors to permeate this or any other house.

She drew smiles from the group when she confessed, "The fact is that I had almost nothing to say about the planning of the kitchen except that I wanted the work space and the sink high enough for me, which was five inches higher than the workmen had ever built one before." The compactness and convenience had been the contribution of the architect, and her only suggestion, she said, was for a pot cupboard because "I am still too modern to want to polish pots and pans for wall decoration." And it was easier, she said, to hop up on a stool and get a quart of tomatoes or a jar of jelly from the nine-foot cupboard shelves than it would have been to go down into a basement, across it, and back up the stairs again for the same errand.

Katherine touched on the small basement, saying, "I was told by everyone that I couldn't do my washing down there. I have found that although there is only room to stand, I always did stand in one spot before, even when I had a huge basement around me.'' She added (this was before clothes dryers became common) that the heat in the small basement made it possible to dry clothes on a portable rack very quickly.

Turning to the rest of the house, Katherine declared that the novel triangular bathtub ''has created more excited comment than the whole house. The neighbor children have been refused winter baths, but have been promised they could come over in their bathing suits in the summer.'' And she added that despite predictions there had been no injuries involving the two brick walls of the bathroom.

She pointed out that the section of cupboards two feet deep, twelve feet long and seven feet high, opposite the kitchen and continuing down the hall from the dining alcove, was ample for all the linen, dishes, cleaning utensils, and extra storage, and even permitted space for a telephone booth. ''This is much envied by women who have children who receive all the telephone calls in the family,'' she said.

''Yes, the house is easy to keep clean,'' Katherine declared, commenting on the queries of visitors. ''Can you imagine not having any dirt from the heating system?'' she asked, reminding her listeners that with the heating pipes laid under the concrete mat, there was no need for hot air registers or radiators. ''It is the most pleasant heat I have ever experienced,'' she said.

The concrete floors are actually a luxury, she continued, saving on work and worry, and easy to clean when waxed or painted. And ''when one gets the inspiration to make some new bedroom furniture or a lamp,'' she said, ''one just rolls back the rug in the living room, brings out saw and hammer, and enjoys all the comforts of home, including the fireplace, while carpentering.'' Thanks to the comfort of floor heating, temperatures could be kept about ten degrees lower than in conventional houses, she asserted.

''I have no curtains to buy, to make or to launder—I have none,'' she boasted. ''The glass doors of the living room and bedrooms have Aeroshades which can be rolled down to give complete privacy or to cut out the sun.'' She went on to point out that the windows were easy to clean with a brush and rubber scraper, and the wood walls, shellacked and waxed, showed no

dirt and caused no ''spring earthquakes'' of painting and papering. Even the brick walls, with their recessed mortar, yielded easily to a once-a-year brushing with the vacuum cleaner.

Not only did she find the storage space adequate, but she did not miss an attic, ''where you put things to their natural death,'' she said. And she ended with this summation:

''I do all my own work for a family of three, washing, ironing, cleaning, baking and sewing, besides showing hundreds of people through the house, explaining and defending it. Still I have time for leisure. A simple, luxurious life in a simple luxurious house.''

''Hundreds of visitors'' was no exaggeration. After the January, 1938 *Archictectural Forum* article the stream increased, from all over the country, and from foreign lands. Why all the interest? Remember that America was just beginning to come out of the Great Depression, with thin purses, but with high hopes for the kind of living that technology had been promising them during the lean years. The magic of Wright's name, plus a price tag that made it all seem possible, were powerful magnets.

We had only been in the house a short time when, in self-protection, we put a sign at the carport, painted in red on a foot-square piece of ceiling board, stating that there was a charge of twenty-five cents to see the house. We loved the house, believed in this kind of architecture, and enjoyed showing it, but thought a sign and charge might cut out the merely curious. Within a few months Katherine found that some Madison women were using the house as a means of entertaining friends instead of an afternoon of bridge, so we doubled the rate to discourage them. We found that it actually saved time to charge. People interested in Wright's architecture appreciated the opportunity, came to look and study, and asked sensible questions. Many of those who came were prospective Wright clients, and they all wanted to know, ''How is he to work with?'' and ''What was the actual cost of the house?''—not believing the published figure.

Workmen and contractors were especially pleasant to encounter, because they spoke a language we were beginning to understand, and because of their enthusiastic comprehension of Wright's daring innovations in simplifying construction. I remember one snowy Sunday when four carpenters and a plumbing-heating man drove three hundred miles through sleet and ice from central Illinois just to look at the house, and went away apparently feeling well rewarded for the trip. Many of the visitors became long-time friends, and some sent back clothing and presents for the children, and even gifts for us. The persons we found it more difficult to show around often had more money than we did and sniffed at the idea of concrete floors, door jambs and window mullions rabbeted out of a two-by-four, the exposed lighting system, and the simple built-in closets.

A gossip columnist for the rival *Wisconsin State Journal* telephoned while we were away on vacation the first year to ask about our house charges. She "expanded" the answer she got from the persons staying in the house while we were gone, and printed a story that the admittance fees had already paid for the entire cost of the house. They did not, of course, but the total for our five years there, I figured, ran to somewhat over five hundred dollars, thus more than covering Wright's fee. (In our second house we were upwardly mobile, charging a dollar and again covering Wright's fee.)

The postman found us too. After the *Forum* article people simply addressed me at Madison, with varied helpful directions. A plumber in Indiana whose tool kit did not include a dictionary put on his envelope, "Lives in Fine New Bungalo." Another person wrote "Newspaperman," and another, "Postmaster: Owner of 1937 modernistic home." A New Jersey teacher anxiously spelled it all out: "Mr. Jacobs lives in house designed by Frank Lloyd Wright, featured in Jan. Architectural Forum."

The most astonishing visitors were engineers flown out that first winter by the giant New York plumbing and heating firm that had withdrawn its offer to participate in the heating experiment. While the men were looking around the living room Katherine left the room for a moment. When she returned she found all four on their hands and knees on the floor, and heard one of them exclaim, "My God, it works!" But they returned to New York and wrote a report declaring that the heating system did not work, we learned later.

Nevertheless, the company wrote asking if they could install monitoring devices to check on the heating efficiency, specifying that I was to run the system at various higher and lower temperatures. "This will consume extra oil, and of course you'll pay for the extra oil?" I asked, just to make sure. "Oh no," they

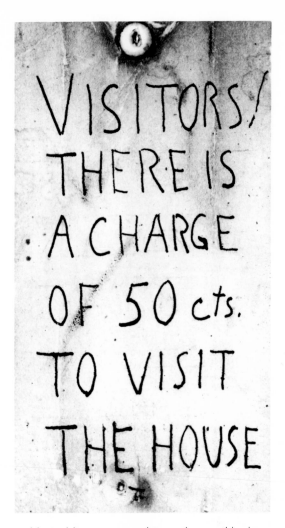

Most visitors appeared to welcome this sign, thumb-tacked to the fulcrum post of the carport, since they felt they were not intruders in asking to see the house. The income from visitors eventually equalled Wright's architectural fee.

Among the dozens who inquired about our Usonian house, there were several who displayed special ingenuity in directing the postman.

Camden County Vocational School
Pennsauken Township, New Jersey

Mr. Herbert Jacobs
Madison, Wisconsin

Mr. Jacobs lives in house
designed by Frank Lloyd Wright,
featured in Jan. Architectural Forum.

Mr Herbert Jacobs

Madison,

Wisconsin.

(Newspaperman)

Plymouth Plumbing & Heating Co.
113 W. LAPORTE STREET
Plymouth, Indiana

Mr. Jacobs.
Madison.
Wisconsin.

Lives in Fine New Bungalo.

52

said. "Then no testing," said I firmly, and that was the end of that. (Perhaps they had been checking on the rumor, relished and relayed to us by a friend in New York, that the house was so cold that my hand had frozen to the wall when I tried to get out of the bathtub.)

Wright stopped by often, usually on his way to view the progress on the Johnson building construction, and he would arrive before eight in the morning, giving notice by rapping smartly on the window with his walking stick. Once he brought his fervent admirer Alexander Woollcott, the drama critic. Katherine, not waiting to hear what pearls might drop from the Woollcott lips, went off to make the bedrooms presentable, but returned in time to hear Wright declare with emphasis, "Alex, *this* is modern architecture." Wright also amused himself by speculating aloud as to how the very fat drama and radio orator would fit in the triangular tub. Their tour continued back through the bedrooms. Katherine had made simple and economical bedspreads out of unbleached muslin, with a monogram. Wright pointed his cane at them and said, "I like that." She was very surprised at the comment, but much pleased, because she valued his opinions.

We had the first of an annual succession of Taliesin parties early in November, 1938, just before they all left for the winter in Arizona. They brought boxes of apples, chunks of firewood, and an enormous pumpkin, all decorated with Wright's trademark of red squares, and many pine boughs for decorating corners and overhangs in the Taliesin style. The fellowship chorus produced roars of laughter from Wright with a parody of "On, Wisconsin," which began "Taliesin, Taliesin, good old shining brow. Run the pencil round the paper, try to please Jack Howe." (John Howe was head draftsman, one of the group of devoted apprentices who slaved long hours to transform Wright's brilliant imaginings into the complicated drawings and perspectives for which Wright was so widely acclaimed. It was no novelty for Jack to be waked up at six in the morning by Wright, who would shout, "Jack, Jack, I've got a great idea here that I want you to get at right away.")

For most of the annual Taliesin parties the group's own chorus sang, but twice I varied the entertainment by reading aloud. One selection was St. Clair McKelway's "An Affix for Birds," from a collection of *New Yorker* magazine short stories. This account of the difficulties of an American in trying to learn the Japanese language especially appealed to Wright because of his four-year stay in Tokyo while building the Imperial Hotel. He borrowed the book (I was never able to get it back) and thereafter regaled Taliesin gatherings with the same tale, laughing so hard himself that he had to make frequent stops.

I have said little about the beauty of the house—a constant delight while living in it—since this is a matter of opinion; but perhaps one indicator will be helpful in understanding the subtleties Wright had created despite the bare minimums of low-cost construction. Both amateur and professional photographers had trouble deciding on just what portions of the house to include in a picture, especially for interior shots. "It doesn't seem to stop anywhere," one person exclaimed. And indeed each segment seemed so well integrated with adjoining areas in Wright's "open plan" that the eye tended to move along a continuous picture. Accustomed to glaring spots of lights from the windows of conventional houses (with the rest of the wall preternaturally dark), we soon came especially to enjoy the soft, even light which came by way of the narrow band of windows just under the roof, a counterpoint to the abundance of light that flooded the whole interior through the glass doors of living room and bedrooms.

The great riches in comfort and beauty that surrounded us made the few drawbacks that appeared seem insignificant. For example, the contrasting boards and battens of the walls furnished such strong emphasis that even the Hiroshigi print from Wright, hung on the wall above that eight-foot living room table, seemed a little uneasy there. I built an easel to display some pictures, but the framed views through the glass doors made pictures for decoration seem unnecessary.

To find any furnishings of simple, good design that suited the house was difficult in those days, when the emphasis was on conventional houses and furnishings. Only very choice, expensive items reflected that quality. Mindful of our rather lightly furnished house, one of the Taliesinites working on the enormous Herbert Johnson home at Racine brought us an inch-thick cast iron shallow bowl nearly two feet wide, which had been rejected because of minor defects as a cover for a huge iron pot to be hung in one of the Johnson fireplaces. Katherine found that it made a handsome receptacle for large branches, or for tall flowers standing in a frog made by boring holes in a wooden pulley the carpenters had discarded. (One day, when Wright suddenly appeared at 7:30 in the morning with four Russian architects in tow, he pointed to a withered arrangement in the bowl and said gently but firmly, "Katherine, you should throw those out.")

On another level, after two winters in the house we were aware that we were not getting the full benefit of the floor heating, because the return pipes were cold to the touch. When we took the problem to Wright, he recommended that the system be changed from steam to forced hot water (a change detailed in the next chapter). Also, on very frigid days, a downdraft from the dining alcove windows proved uncomfortable for those sitting on the bench built against the wall. Storm windows there and for all the major expanses of glass would have helped, but we felt we could not afford them. I cured most of the downdraft at the dining table by making a small three-panel standing screen, covered with burlap. I should point out that sweaters and a roaring fire in very cold weather were a tradeoff that we gladly paid in exchange for the year-round delight to the eye of the glass walls of living room and bedroom, and for the lower cost of a small heating system. And we were young, buoyant and active. Had we been old we doubtless would have been uncomfortable at times.

We found much to enjoy and appreciate in the whole house, but we especially enjoyed the fireplace. It was not the dinky little aperture of some dwellings, crouched under an overburdened mantel, and hiding behind a brass screen or even a glass window prison, but a large, boldly stated fireplace Wright designed to be the very heart and symbol of the home. We had not even imagined the pleasure, for instance, of a hob, enabling one to sit almost on top of the fire and bake. And to be near the fire and watch a snowstorm swirling around the windows was especially satisfying. I am aware that engineers gravely assert that fireplaces, unless provided with special heat exchange devices, are inefficient to the point of drawing in so much cold air that they neutralize the effect of the heat they give out. I do not believe, however, that they pay sufficient attention to the radiation effect of a fireplace. People sitting in front of one are cheered by the sight of the blaze, and

directly warmed by the heat waves radiated from the fire. If their backs happen to be nestled in a large chair, they are quite comfortable. "I have always tried to have important meetings around a fireplace," Allen Dulles said once. "There is some subtle influence in a wood fire which makes people feel at ease and less inhibited in their conversations."

That massive fireplace, the brick piers and the cement floor combined also to create a "thermal mass" which helped to equalize temperatures, especially in the hot, humid days of a Midwest summer. They retained enough coolness from the night, aided by air currents from the many windows, to keep the house from being stiflingly hot.

With his experience of the Taliesin group growing most of its own food, Wright had emphasized a big garden as one of the economies of the house. I could understand, because as a youth I had participated, not too eagerly, in helping to plant, cultivate by hand, and harvest vegetables from almost two acres of garden for the summer camp that was part of the social settlement run by my parents. But it would be different, working my own land for myself, and we went at it with enthusiasm. That first summer, while the house was building, I had spaded up a few square feet "just to try it out," but the pitiful results—a few radishes and a couple of handfuls of beans—did not discourage me. In our first full year, 1938, we cultivated a plot that measured about twenty by eighty feet, and my records show that for about four dollars' worth of seed we cut our grocery bills from an average of seven dollars a week (please remember that these were Depression prices) to four dollars a week during the summer, besides canning hundreds of quarts for the winter. I tried for two crops over most of the garden, experimented with new kinds of vegetables and different varieties of old ones, and tried my hand, with only partial success, at transplanting things like parsnips, carrots and beets.

As my mother had done, following in the steps of her own mother, who had started one in 1860, the year of her marriage, I kept a "Garden Book" to record the dates of plantings, what did well and what should be changed next year; it soon came to include a diary-like account of trips taken, parties given, and weather and bird observations. As the children grew older, they were encouraged to write in it great events like the first bicycle ride

The bank of door-windows which formed the east wall of the living room framed a view of the distant hills. The shrub hedge bordering the property had just begun to grow when this picture was taken. (Photo by Herbert Jacobs)

alone, sightings of meadowlarks, and other significant vital statistics. And I found the Garden Book and its successors full of dates and details of changes made in the house that aided me in composing this account.

The border of shrubs around the two outside edges of the land which we planted that first spring—lilacs, mock orange, snowball, Russian olive, bridal wreath, syringa, all the old classics—came on famously by the second year, and we felt ourselves walled in, living in our own private world. We were less successful with trees: we put in too many, and they grew too big. At first we were delighted when the three apple trees managed sparse clumps of blossoms by the third year, but the pines we put in seemed to stand still. (Years later, when we drove by the house, we saw our mistake in planting conifers that grew to be giants, too close to the building. The sun, view and light that had been among our chief delights were now obscured in a perpetual gloom of branches.)

I will not claim that the house spurred me along the path of civic activity, but it did serve ably as a place for gatherings. First I led a movement for extension of the bus line to our area. Then, in-

censed when I discovered that the telephone company charged us a higher rate just because we were not within the corporate city limits—while some residents of the city, living farther away from the center than we did, paid the lower city rate—I inaugurated a petition to the public service commission to bracket us in the city rate. We won our case, but in the process the ingenious phone company lawyers transformed our minuscule matter into a counter-demand for a state-wide rate boost, so our net gain was nil.

I rallied people for school board meetings to lower our suburban tuition rates (we won), and circulated many a petition for causes which seemed terribly important then, although I cannot now remember the subjects. We filled the living room with folding chairs borrowed from a local church for a meeting to organize a community association, which I headed for two years; and when we entered World War II, I became the air raid warden for the area in that footless effort of the civil defense authorities to keep the minds of the populace occupied. Thanks to my vigilant eye, not one bomb fell on or near us.

Like many another newly built suburb, ours was largely composed of young married couples with growing children. Strongly conscious of our duties as well as our rights, we and our neighbors bustled into many a cause which we hoped would improve our lives and our neighborhood. Many of our friends and neighbors were teaching at the university, or in one of the state government departments. And most of us were there for the same basic reasons: more room to live, and lower costs while our children were growing up.

I had the pleasure, during those first years in the house, of "correcting" the august *New York Times,* and of sticking the wealthy *Time Magazine* for a handful of snapshots. Such golden moments come rarely to reporters from the provinces. The *Times* had carried a long article on Wright by English architectural critic Geoffrey Baker, who managed to include a few swipes at our house for what he called its crudities of construction, and what he said was the "failure" of the heating system—all this, so far as I know, without seeing the house. Indignantly, I sent off a long reply to the *Times,* and for good measure demanded payment for my letter, on the ground that the paper's printing of all those errors by the critic had taken a lot of my time and energy to correct. To my delight the *Times* sent me a fifteen-dollar check, which would seem to disprove the paper's claims that it never, but never, pays for letters.

The encounter with *Time Magazine* came about because of an over-zealous advertising manager. *Architectural Forum* had printed a double run, totalling 120,000 copies of the *Forum* issue devoted to Wright, thinking the extra copies would sell readily, but sales were slow. Advertisements in *Time* offering the extra copies had featured a picture of Fallingwater, but someone at *Time* noticed that fully half the queries they received were about our house. The advertising manager told of this in a letter to me, and asked me to lend *Time* "a few snapshots" so that they could feature my house in some ads, instead of Fallingwater. Reflecting on *Time's* reputation for tossing money around, and on my own meager finances, I wrote that I would sell, not lend, five snapshots. *Time* sent me fifty dollars. Then, a few months later, came a letter from *Time*, asking me why I had sent the pictures. It developed that the advertising manager with the bright idea had disappeared through the revolving door which seems to be waiting for many of them, and his puzzled successor had different thoughts. So they kept the pictures and I kept the fifty dollars.

Sometimes our bits of extra income came through what one might call "affirmative economy." When several young friends said they wished they could cook as cheaply and yet as tastefully as Katherine, she wrote and we mimeographed a cookbook in card file form, with a month's menus added stressing dishes from leftovers. After distributing as wedding presents more than a dozen in hand-lettered ten-cent tin boxes we sold the rest through a local department store at a good profit above all costs.

9.

The Picture Changes

During those first two or three years we were having a wonderful time, relishing the beauty and convenience of the house, getting used to a radically different style of living, and basking in the enthusiasm of visitors and friends, for it was a lovely place in which to entertain. From being spectators we became participants, cautiously suggesting minor alterations, and going along with Wright in an upgrading of both house and heating system.

We were pleased when many young architects came to see and learn, and we put on a knowing smile for the standard remark of their older confreres, "There are some things I like about this house—and some things I don't!" With the overconfidence of amateurs, we freely aired our views, even though they were not based on any profound knowledge.

Wright had started receiving many commissions for Usonian houses, and since ours was already in existence, he brought or sent some clients to us to get an idea of what was in store for them. We felt like midwives to modern architecture. One client whom Wright brought to us himself was Loren Pope, the Washington newsman who later built at Falls Church, Virgina. (The house is now owned by the National Trust for Historic Preservation and, because of an earlier change of owners, now called the Pope-Leighey house.) Charles "Fritz" Manson of Wausau, Wisconsin, saw our house, liked it, and went to Wright for one of his own, later becoming a close friend. Another client was Lloyd Lewis, the Civil War historian and Chicago newspaperman. Wright had employed him in the late 1920s as a "negative press agent," to keep Wright's name out of the paper at a time of extreme personal difficulties, but of course Wright could not resist sounding off to any reporter, so the arrangement did not last. Lewis, who would

soon build his own Wright house, came on a Sunday afternoon when Katherine and I were both holding up boards above our heads, paneling the ceiling in a pattern designed by Wright, and I always regretted that I thought I was too busy on the ladder to come down and talk to him. I lost a bet with Wright on one timid Wisconsin client who plagued me for months with his questions and worries. I wagered that he would never actually build, but he did, and I had to settle the bet with ten pounds of good aged cheese for the Taliesin Fellowship.

An incident in the spring of 1939 showed the ruggedness of Wright's construction, and how luck can rule our lives. We were lounging on the terrace on a Sunday afternoon when I heard a terrific bang from the front of the house. When I rushed there, I could not open the screen door, because the car of my neighbor from across the street was jammed alongside it. The brake had been improperly set, and the car had rolled down his driveway and across the street, knocking out the fulcrum of two-by-fours which supported the cantilever of the carport roof. This slowed it down some, before it hit the brick wall of the bathroom.

The miracle to me was that our five-year-old daughter Susan had been playing in that spot in the carport just a few minutes before, but had come into the house to get something. My neighbor, himself a building contractor, was already beside his car by the time I ran around to the other door. He was trying to disentangle the smashed lumber of the fulcrum, but I yelled at him, "Get a prop under the outside corner of the roof." That roof, fully sixteen feet wide, was largely supported by two flitch plates (planks bolted together with a steel plate between them), anchored to steel rods buried deep in the brick wall which formed one side of the carport. The flitch plates got their bearing from the fulcrum, three feet from the wall. The neighbor and I put a post under the corner, and found his car had done no damage to the bathroom or carport walls. But, having young children of his own, he turned a shade whiter when I told him about my daughter's close call. He looked at the plans, and put in a new fulcrum the next day.

What surprised and pleased me about Wright's architecture was that the bathroom brick wall withstood the impact of the heavy car, and even more remarkable, the carport roof sagged less than a foot when its main support was knocked out. Years later one of

"Usonia No. 1," Frank Lloyd Wright's answer to the challenge of low-cost housing, "turns its back on the street" and emphasizes its close relation to the ground with the horizontal lines of the board-and-batten walls. The living room is at right, and the bedroom wing extends at left behind the overhang of the carport. (Photo by Larry Cuneo)

the succession of new owners built a corner support for the carport roof. I believe, but do not know, that when the fulcrum was knocked out it strained the tie rods in the brick wall, weakening the brick anchor.

The reason that our own car was not damaged in this incident was that we no longer had one. I had sold it to pay doctor and hospital bills for the delivery of our second child, and I was riding the four miles to the office on a bicycle, and taking a bus in winter. We got on well without a car, thanks to a good grocery store three blocks away, and my discovery that I could carry big loads (including my daughter) on the handlebar basket of the bicycle. I used to brag that the most exciting fifteen minutes of my life was when I carried two unsecured four-foot squares of plywood on my bicycle in a high wind. We leaned on friends for transport, and the Wrights even sent in apprentices to pick us up for parties.

We did not feel deprived: just the opposite. Our friends envied us our luxurious life in that house. We just didn't have much money to spend on other things. We were a bit outside the American pattern, anyway. We had no charge accounts or other installment payments besides the mortgage; and I found that my salary, then about forty-two dollars a week, was enough to carry that and other living expenses. We bore down heavily on the garden, trying to get two and even three crops during the growing season, and even taking on the adjacent vacant lot for additional garden. We also saved money by rolling our own cigarets—using a five-cent bag, good for forty cigarets, called "Golden Grain," which looked and smelled something like tobacco, but I believe did not actually carry that word on the label—and we celebrated with an occasional swig of cheap sherry from a gallon jug.

In addition to the mishap to the carport, several other matters during 1939 gradually educated us to the fact that we were living in an experimental as well as beautiful house. One was the heating system, so novel that no one, including Wright, really knew how it would work, or what bugs would be found in it. One of the brick piers in the living room needed correction, because of my negligence in failing to provide sufficient ground fill in the terrace extension at the south end of the living room. And Wright, seeing the house the center of so many eyes, naturally wanted to make it more attractive with a paneled ceiling covering the fiberboard, and a better quality of wood for the outside fascias. Step by step we met the problems and the proposed solutions, even enjoying the learning process, in spite of the financial pinch.

The heating system, contrary to our too-early boasts, had not been entirely successful. The original layout called for four two-inch pipes to circle the living room, and three pipes to do the same for the bedroom wing, with steam pressure of zero to five pounds. We learned later that steam follows the hottest pipe. When the furnace started up at the end of a sunny day, the first pipe in the living room would get hot, then gradually the other three, one after the other. And after those four pipes it was the turn of the bedroom pipes. Thus most of the time we were not getting the benefit of full radiation from all the pipes. Even at full operation the return ends of the pipes remained cool, when they should have been too hot to touch. The bathroom, with no special heating unit and with two outside uninsulated walls, was chilly. The farthermost bedroom, served by only one loop of pipes, was definitely cold, but we didn't care because we never used it in winter. A portable electric-steam radiator that we tried proved too noisy for bedroom or living room, so we used it in the bathroom.

The same type of floor heating system had been installed in the Johnson administration building and in Johnson's home, but there the steam was under seventy pounds of pressure, and the pipes reportedly kept grass green up to four feet from the walls all winter. Steam for our size house had simply not been the right answer. We called in a Madison "heating expert," but the best he could come up with was a suggestion to put big blowers in the living room and the bedroom hallway, which sounded horrible. So we did what we should have done earlier—put the problem up to Wright. He suggested changing the system to forced hot water, which he was already specifying in the second generation of Usonian houses. This plan was carried out by Hugh Peake, the original plumber and heating man, on two mild days in February, 1940. After this change, all the pipes got hot at once, with a lower water temperature. The drop in temperature of the return pipes was insignificant, and the system gave us much-improved heating in normal weather. In very cold weather—ten or fifteen below zero with a strong wind—the heating system was not big enough to combat the heat loss of the large glass areas and the only average insulation, though sweaters and a fire in the fireplace kept us quite comfortable. We also added a radiator in the bathroom.

When we converted to forced hot water, we also changed from oil to coal, still trying to economize wherever we could. (Coal was no hardship for me to handle. I had been raised in the twenty-seven room Settlement House in Milwaukee, and as soon as I found myself as tall as a shovel, I was put in charge of the heating, shoveling forty tons of coal every winter, plus what seemed to be an equal quantity of ashes.) Actually the change in heating proved a minor expense, and I built the coal bin myself, supplied by an outside chute. Storm windows would have helped our house too; I believe later owners added them.

That Leaning-Tower-of-Pisa pier at the south end of the living room—in reality less than three inches off plumb—was more annoying. The plans had called for a sodded terrace going out about twenty feet at the same level as the house, but I had neglected to provide the needed fill. Grove, the contractor, warned me of probable trouble unless I finished the terrace with more dirt, but I couldn't bear to think of more expense and inconvenience, so I did nothing. The slight tilt was beginning to strain the cross bars in the slot windows. The plans had also called for a fence extending from the pier along the center of the terrace, to continue the board and batten pattern of the walls, but when the tilt began, I decided to wait until that was cured. When I finally built the fence, a year later, I realized again the importance of carrying out Wright's plans to completion to achieve his desired effects. The fence turned the garden side into our own private walled enclosure, extending the sense of space and relating the house even better to the earth.

Here are a couple of paragraphs from a two-page letter of mine to Wright which show how we felt about the house changes—and the need for continued economy:

"First of all, let me assure you again, if it is necessary, that we are not planning any changes you don't approve of. We were much touched by your offer to advance the money for whatever changes are made, but we're not going to accept it. It just wouldn't be fair, after all you've done for us, to ask you to raise money to correct things which were left out because of our own original price limitations. I am quite certain that I can borrow the money, and I will do this.

"As to the inside covering on the ceiling, I'd like to offer some suggestions. You mentioned plywood, perhaps in the pattern of the walls. I wonder whether straight boards and battens, such as are now in the walls, might not be as effective, and I believe they would be cheaper. I wonder also whether I couldn't put most of this ceiling on myself. I have two free days a week, you know, besides evenings, and am not unacquainted with carpentry. You have doubtless guessed already that what I am after is to keep the cost as low as possible. As Katherine says, 'We work so hard for what money we have; why not do as much of the work as we can ourselves?' "

I mentioned several other very minor house ailments which had come to light, but ended the letter on an affirmative note:

"I am afraid after reading all the above, that you will feel we are blue and discouraged about the house. The reverse is true. We are still delighted with it, and haven't any really fundamental complaints."

Wright answered in one of his brief letters that he "admired and appreciated" our attitude, that he would keep the cost below five hundred dollars, and that pine boards and battens would be all right for the ceiling. Within ten days Herbert Fritz, young Taliesin apprentice and later architect practicing in Madison and Spring Green, arrived to rebuild the pier. We provided board and room, and he rapidly rebuilt the pier, jacked up the slanting concrete of the last few feet of terrace, stuffed dirt under it, and replaced the crumbling fireplace bricks. Two other Taliesin apprentices spent a day showing me how to put the boards and battens on the underside of the roof, inside and out. I had hoped that they would stay around long enough to do all the outside overhangs, instead of retreating to more interesting work at Taliesin after placing about four boards, but I hoped in vain. At least, since we no longer had a car, we could store the boards under shelter in the carport, rather than filling the living room with them.

Naturally the new burst of activity called for a party, so we had the second annual Taliesin gathering October 15, 1939. In true

The fence hiding the garden from the street was covered with vines, and the border of shrubs had grown high when this picture was taken in about 1950. (Photo by Herbert Jacobs)

down-to-the-wire Taliesin style, some of them came early, helping to clean up the last of the carpentry and masonry debris just minutes before the rest of the group arrived at the front door for an evening of dinner and music. (And it was months before we found everything that our helpers had tucked away.)

Wright took time out from the party to instruct me in my first use of a caulking gun. I was trying very hard to get the thinnest possible line of caulking compound into the crack where brick and glass joined at the slot windows, but Wright, superintending my labors, said: "Herbert, that's not the way to use a machine-age tool. Pour it out in one continuous wide bead." I had been trying to save caulking compound, but Wright, the long-time advocate of machine use in building, knew that saving time, rather than trying to economize on basically cheap materials, represented the true road to building economy. (He was thinking in general terms, because in the particular instance, my own time was free.) Following his instruction, I gave hearty squeezes to the handle of the caulking gun, pouring out a thick gray caterpillar of compound, much wider than my original efforts, but actually neater looking. "That's the way!" Wright said approvingly.

A handful of our developing friends among the apprentices stayed after the party to help wash dishes and clean up. (We never did, over all the years, manage to acquire a dishwashing machine—in fact didn't even think about one.) We had come to know nearly all the apprentices by sight, through seeing them on their educational visits to our house and on our frequent trips to Taliesin during the first year or two. During the mid-thirties Taliesin regularly offered a Sunday afternoon movie, plus a cup of tea and piece of cake, as a lure to possible clients, and as a way of integrating the new Taliesin Fellowship, established in 1932, into the Madison and Wisconsin scene. The movie was always a foreign import, and for fifty cents the visitor got not only movie, cake and tea, but a glimpse of the master himself. Wright managed always to wander for a few moments through the audience, nodding briefly and then vanishing.

After we had established ourselves in the house we found ourselves going to Taliesin more frequently, but for pleasure now rather than business. We made costumes and joined a Halloween masked ball, attended many a dress-up Sunday evening dinner and musical in the Wrights' living room, and enjoyed an occa-

sional weekend there relaxing without the children. Often we were invited to join the fellowship for their regular Sunday noon picnics, held on wooded, rocky outlooks above the nearby valleys. Wright's favorite place he had named Borglum Rocks, in honor of the big-thinking sculptor who carved boldly with dynamite at Mt. Rushmore.

A gift from Herbert (Hib) Johnson, head of the wax firm, also pleased him at this time, gratifying his interest in using machines. The gift, a deluxe phonograph and record changer, piped music not only to all the workrooms, but outdoors as well. During its first novel months Wright often abruptly changed records that had scarcely begun to play, as he walked about the studio or talked to visitors, by pressing control buttons on a long black cord that he trailed behind him.

During the rest of the fall and winter, with Katherine's help, I continued slowly, paneling the ceiling in the pattern Wright had laid out. I learned the hard way, by having boards fall on my head, that it's a good idea to support sixteen-foot boards on both ends, and probably in the middle too, if one intends to fit them into the batten grooves—and have them stay in place long enough to drive home a few two-and-a-half-inch cadmium-plated screws. I had no miter box, but learned to become rather fair at marking a forty-five-degree angle with a T-square and sawing, where the pattern turned corners. We spent most of the winter on the paneling, including the overhangs—more than enough to convince me that the house was really quite large. (Taliesin put the square footage at 2,200 feet, which I believe included half the overhang.)

Wright had stressed the insulating value of sheathing the ceiling with an added layer of wood, but probably the aesthetic effect he sought was even more dominant. The fiberboard ceiling, despite its rectangular pattern, looked—and was—cheap. The pattern he evolved for the ceiling, with the boards and battens echoing the strong horizontal lines of the walls, transformed the surface into an aesthetic pleasure to the eye—just as the edging of bricks around the mat, the slot windows, and the overhang of the bathroom roof made the difference between common and distinguished.

Wright was still experimenting. Taliesin had developed a new kind of roof covering bearing the felicitous name "Wearcoat," which from Wright's description sounded almost as tough as armor plate. Would we try it, at a token price? After such a siren description, who could resist, even though the roof covering was less than three years old? And for dressier appearance, Wright wanted new fascia boards of redwood, wider and thicker than the cheap-looking boards then in place, which had a tendency to curl because they were so thin and could not be nailed close to their edges. I put on the fascia board in the spring of 1940, after completing all the ceiling paneling, inside and out. It was easy on the seven-foot-high bedroom wing, but a lot more of a sporting proposition on the nine-foot living room exterior, balancing on the top step of my five-foot stepladder, and using a brace and bit to drill holes and sink the long screws.

Naturally that luxurious redwood fascia, nearly two inches thick, was made to produce an extra dividend. We sanded and waxed one sawed-off end and bored five holes down the center, to make a candelabra for the big living room table for Christmas and other festive occasions, for which it continues to serve us. And with some of the boards and battens left over from the ceiling paneling I built a low storage cupboard, patterned to match the wall, on part of the outside of the bedroom corridor, for winter storage of all the door screens. For the first two years we had stored them in the seldom-used last bedroom. I was able to add the five hundred dollars or so of extra cost of all these changes on to the mortgage.

The spirit of changing things became rampant and infectious. Katherine wanted more light shining down on all the good food she put on that sociable dining table. She experimented with extra concealed lights in the "catwalk," the extension of the seven-foot bedroom roof height which ran above the table, finally designing a triangular-patterned grid which I then made. Wright said it looked good when I installed the lights behind these small wooden grids.

I tried my hand at more furniture, bolting maple arms and a back to a steel studio couch frame, in a style which I flattered myself was similar to that of the large easy chairs made by the Wescott cousins. With cushions added, this bed transformed into a couch served well as something to pull up to the fireplace when we were entertaining, and performed the same service ably in the second Wright house. I had to reinforce the bottom years later, but it was still going strong after more than twenty years' service.

10.

Flight From Paradise

My entries in the Garden Book were the soul of brevity. On September 6, 1942 I wrote: "We are talking of selling our house and moving to a farm near Madison. Have been out twice so far to look at one 52-acre farm."

Friends did not even try to conceal their shock when they learned that, having finally completed our lovely house, we were selling it to move to a rundown farm and lead a much more strenuous life in an ugly, inconvenient dwelling. "How can you bear to leave all this?" was their refrain. We wondered ourselves, although in fact we were already expecting to build soon a new Wright house on the farm's hilltop site, having picked the farm with that site in mind.

Katherine and I tend to make up our minds fast, and then to act immediately. The next Garden Book entry, November 26—Thanksgiving Day—after naming the house buyer and farm seller, merely stated: "We moved to the farm Nov. 13, being much surprised that we had so many possessions to take with us." I can flesh out that brief record with details published less than five years after the event, rather than looking back in rosy recollection. Writing has always been my trade, and I found that I made much more money describing farming and rural life than I produced by my rather haphazard activities as a part-time farmer. The first of a succession of publications was a book, *We Chose the Country* (Harper's, 1948). Here is part of what I wrote, which of course also embodied the insights and suggestions of Katherine:

"With gardening in the summer, and bragging about it during the winter, while loafing around the big fireplace, we had as pleasant a life as anyone could wish, but we were beginning to be vaguely dissatisfied, without knowing just why. Our life in the Wright house probably contributed to this unrest. The banks of floor-to-ceiling windows on the garden side made nature a great part of the house, letting in the sun, the moon and the stars, adding the changing landscape as a permanent part of our daily life. It renewed in us the love of the out-of-doors which we had both known before we entered an adult, urban life. Neither of our family backgrounds had taught us to enjoy the luxuries of the city, with business and social success the goal, and bridge parties for recreation.

"In Katherine's early life, as the youngest of six children, raised on a picturesque but not too productive farm in the kettle moraine area of central Wisconsin, the wonders and beauties of nature were the luxuries of life. We had no hayloft stage or bird-calling father in my own youth, but the Settlement House's summer camp furnished an acceptable substitute, with lake and woods—in spite of an occasional touch of too much garden.

"Our trips to Taliesin to see Wright probably played a part too. What had started as an architect-client relationship grew into an easy friendship which led us out there often for Sunday musicals by the apprentices, and for other events. The drive itself, down the dramatic Wisconsin River valley, with its high bluffs on either side, always delighted us, and to spend a few hours in the center of those wonderful hills and valleys, walking under great trees or looking out across the river valley through the big windows, added to the thrill. On those visits we always marveled at the prodigal way in which growing things were cut and brought into the house to enhance the architectural beauty—great branches of oak trees, or long sections of grapevine. What struck us repeatedly was the bounty that lay at hand in the country, ready for whoever chose to take it.

"Against this background of vague discontent we began reading the books. You know the kind I mean—those that sing of the delights of the country from a snug retreat on Fifth Avenue. They tell you how easy and pleasant it all is, and by the time they are through with their witchery, you can almost smell the apple blossoms as the cows come up the lane, every animal docile and beautiful, each anxious to pour out two pails full of nothing but rich cream.

"E.B. White's "One Man's Meat" was undoubtedly the worst

in its effect on us. This sensitive New Yorker, at that time transplanted to a salt-water farm in Maine, writing witty dispatches from the lamb and chicken front, set Katherine and me in a seething ferment of country love.

"In contrast to this romanticizing was the calculating fellow who had it all figured out to the last nut and bolt. You needed exactly four hundred dollars worth of tools, nails, nuts and screws to start out with, and just so many pigs, no more, no less, or you couldn't be a subsistence farmer and make a go of it . . . .

"Of course the mere reading of three or four books was not enough to make us jump to the country in one bound, but probably it played a large part in causing us to sit up and reappraise our living experience. We took stock to see whether we were getting as much solid satisfaction out of life as these carolers of country joys seemed to be. We began to wonder whether in the city we ever could succeed in fitting our desires to our income—to take time for friendships, instead of begrudging the long moments consumed by acquaintances and idlers; to insure ourselves space and privacy; to dig our hands into the bounty of food and freedom that is not found in city streets.

"In the back of our minds had been the idea that 'some day,' probably when the children had grown up and departed, we would move out into a rural nook, but there seemed to be no pressing hurry. Nevertheless, we scanned the children, and the life they were living—and making us lead—with a closer eye. Susan was then seven years old, a roly-poly, pigtailed blue-eyed stargazer who was showing real talent with her first whack at the piano and with the crayon drawings that most children between six and eight seem to be able to dash off with grace and interest—before formal education grabs hold of them. Elizabeth, a curly-headed dumpling of three, had reached the age of cooky mooching from door to door without parental supervision.

"Like all the rest of our neighbors with a city growing up around us, we seemed to be spending more and more of our time thinking up harmless and mildly educational activities to keep our children out of mischief. Sometimes it seemed like a full-time job for one person just to superintend two small and reasonably well-behaved children. Now if we were only on a farm, we thought, the children could be playing with animals, doing chores, or working

The barn and high silo of the farm were a frequent scene of activity, especially for the children. Here the small herd of cows gleans among old cornstalks. The farmhouse is almost concealed at far right beyond the haystack. (Photo by Herbert Jacobs)

at interesting tasks beside us, instead of just getting in our hair all the time.

"It has struck me since that formal education may be overlooking animals as one of the great motivating forces of children. After all, the books children take most delight in are about animals . . . and besides, animals aren't always giving orders.

"The fact that the city was crowding in on all sides of us also played a part. When we built the house it stood in open fields, and it simply never occurred to us that some day the Depression-cursed stretch of barren stakes might come to life with a vengeance. Soon, through the huge bank of glass doors that formed one wall of the living room, we could see little boxes of houses springing up all around us, and it was no longer open country. We were becoming surrounded by people with whom we had no more in common than a back fence . . .

"In the space of less than two months we had made up our

minds, bought a fifty-two-acre farm on a high plateau just nine miles west of the center of Madison, sold our house, and jumped to the country. Katherine says it's like getting on a roller coaster. You know there are a lot of thrills and chills ahead—some magnificent heights and some awful drops—but you have decided to do it. Before you know it you are in the car and moving, and then there is no turning back."

We had sold the furniture with the house, and did all our moving with a decrepit bakery truck, which I had bought for $135 and converted with a coat of red paint and the cutting of two small windows in the sides. When the final load trundled out, and the elegant house was bare, there were some tears and heartaches, mingled with the expectations of a new venture. Wright was vastly disappointed at our disposing of the house, though somewhat mollified at our announced determination to build anew on the farm hilltop.

Just before we moved, he called for us with his car to drive to Taliesin, and we had him swing past the farm and its hilltop so that he could get an idea of the splendors which were possible. The farm had a long, low barn, dwarfed by a concrete silo more than twice the height of the barn. Pointing to the high silo, I said lightly, "I'm thinking of calling the place Phallic Pharm." Still brooding over our traitorous act in selling "his" house, Wright shot back, "You mean Fallacy Farm!" He did show a little interest in the hilltop, but I believe he felt we would rusticate into feckless rural incompetents, never to surface again as clients.

Part Two

THE SOLAR HEMICYCLE

II.

Tasting a Different Life

Although Wright showed a flicker of interest in the proposed building site in a high field overlooking miles of rolling hills, he also glanced at the unprepossessing farmhouse, barn and other buildings. Perhaps he asked himself whether we were worth designing a home for again, if we could live in a place like that after being exposed for five years to the marvels he had created. But on our side we were mindful that this was the only farm we had been able to discover near enough to my job in the city, with an attractive building site, and at a price we could afford.

Within three weeks after that hurried drive-past with Wright we had left our beautiful little house and plunged into the strenuous and unfamiliar career of part-time farmers. We were buoyed by the excitement of a new adventure and the bubbling enthusiasm of the children for a life in the country with animals, but as parents we realized some of the hazards and pitfalls ahead. What we did not fully appreciate was how jumping with both feet into this new world would change our attitudes and way of life—and greatly increase the skills and strength we would need later when we started actual building.

Katherine's first reaction to the dirt and mess of the neglected farmhouse was, "I can live in the barn, but not the house." When we took on the formidable task of cleaning and painting to make it liveable by our city standards we thought that World War II would soon be over and we could be building again. But the war went on and on, and it was four years before we could even start to build on that glorious hilltop.

Like a swimmer testing the water with one toe I began slowly, gradually acquiring more animals and the chores that went with them, soon building up with overconfidence until I had more than I could handle, and then speedily cutting back to a level I could manage. But first we had our hands full just making the filthy farmhouse fit to live in. We began while still in the Wright house, with the purchase of the aged bakery panel truck to get us out and back to the farm—cheap because its tires were paper-thin. Every time we dashed out to the farm, on Sundays and my days off, we suffered one or more flat tires, though by some magic Katherine when alone could whizz around the countryside and never suffer a single flat. The restrictions of World War II were already in force, but as a prospective "farmer" I was entitled to priorities for tires. This turned out to be merely a hunting license, and it took four weeks, enlivened by ten flats in twelve days, before I could lay my hands on a set of four shoddy recaps.

With both gas and oil stoves rationed off the market, we bought a huge coal and wood cooking stove from a retired farm wife, and a washing machine that she claimed was worth an extra five dollars on the ground that it was historic, having been used to

The standard pattern of barn, chicken house, windmill and farm-house appears here. The house is deceptively new looking, despite its eighty years, thanks to its outside shell of asbestos siding. The windmill was later taken down and sections of it were used for reinforcement in the concrete cover of the dry well. (Photo by Herbert Jacobs)

make butter during one of Wisconsin's milk strikes—which I had covered as a reporter.

Fortunately, Katherine had been raised on a farm and knew how to cook and live with a wood and coal stove. We banked it with coal to keep it going all night, for the cookstove and a small oil-fired space heater in the living room which we had bought from the shiftless farm tenant were our only sources of heat. A foot-square register in the floor of the bedroom above took a bit of the chill off that room for the children, but our downstairs small bedroom had to make do with whatever heat seeped around the corner from the living room.

The oil heater set the old chimney afire now and then, and Katherine swears that on cold nights she slept with one eye open, ready to seize and use the can of chemical compound which sat beside the stove for the extinguishing of such blazes. The children, indifferent to fire hazards, found the register in the bedroom floor ideal for passing messages up and down on a string, but were even more delighted with the opening in the floor of the bedroom above the kitchen stove, covered merely by a board, where a small basket could be raised or lowered. The high point for them came when my father, who sometimes occupied the upstairs bedroom during the summer, fell asleep while napping with his watch in his hand, and dropped it, with disastrous results, when he relaxed. They were even more fascinated by the hand-cranked wall telephone. We had eleven other families on our party line, and they all listened in every time it rang.

We had bought merely the land and buildings, so at the farm auction of machinery, feed and livestock, just before we moved, we acquired cheaply some unusable farm machinery, plus a barn-full of hay, great quantities of oats and baled straw, and a dozen acres of standing field corn, still on the stalks and waiting to be harvested. We were so terrified at the mysteries and confusion of our first farm auction that we did not attempt to bid on any of the dozen cows in the barn. At that time I did not even know how to milk, a fact unknown to Katherine. I cured this ignorance almost immediately by paying an overnight visit to my brother's farm a few miles away, while Katherine took a week's trip to visit her family, at their large farm in New Jersey.

One pig and a dozen chickens, bought from the tenant whose messy house we had had to clean and paint, constituted our total animal investment when we started living on the farm in the middle of November, 1942. In the good old farm tradition, water had been piped to the barn but not to the house. A local plumber connected us to the pump in the center of the barnyard, but we could not use the water until I could lay my hands on a tank to store it in. This time priorities were no help, and tanks were simply unavailable—at least to strangers in the community. Then I happened to pass a bakery which advertised fifty-gallon fat cans for sale. I bought one, Katherine scoured it with appropriate cleaning fluids, and a local farm repair shop soldered in an outlet pipe. Placed in a spare bedroom above the kitchen sink, the tank served faithfully until the war ended and pressure tanks became once more available.

I cite the water tank as one example of the many makeshifts and inconveniences we encountered, sometimes ruefully but mostly with enthusiasm and an occasional bit of ingenuity. Building kitchen cabinets and counters, partitions in the kitchen lean-to for washbowl, makeshift shower and "carryout" toilet, plus more carpenter work in barn, chicken house and a dozen other places gave me experience and confidence when it finally came time to tackle finishing the interior of the new Wright house.

Well before Christmas that first year we acquired a couple of cows, and I found myself boosting the children up to the haymow to "help" pitch down hay. To handle the accumulation of manure, I nailed a curl of stovepipe to an old piece of plywood, creating a tobaggan or light stoneboat with which to haul it out to the fields. For fifteen dollars one of our new neighbors sold me an elderly mare named Lu to pull the tobaggan and furnish an occasional ride for the children. Lu also pulled the balky truck when it refused to start on very cold mornings—activities which postponed her inevitable visit to the fox farm by nearly two years. She tired so easily that sometimes she sat down on the hood of the car, but she could manage a trot, and sometimes even a brief gallop when I covered the manure with straw to give the children a ride out and back through the snow.

With plenty of good Jersey milk available from our own cow, Katherine started making butter and cottage cheese, and superb pancakes from the buttermilk, in addition to her long-time bread making. Naturally, with all the milking, carpentering and other farm activities my appetite increased tremendously—and so did

Son William, nearly two years old, gets the traditional Saturday-nighter beside the big kitchen stove. (Photo by Herbert Jacobs)

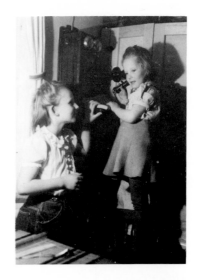

Susan (left) and Elizabeth try out the hand-cranked telephone. Eleven other farm families shared the rural line— and many of them listened in, every time it rang. (Photo by Herbert Jacobs)

Lu, the fifteen-dollar horse, is hitched in this picture to a light farm wagon called a democrat. Elizabeth and Susan took turns driving, and Lu's age meant that there was never any danger of a runaway. (Photo by Katherine Jacobs)

Father and son, in the farm driveway, ready for the evening's milking and other chores. (Photo by Katherine Jacobs)

my weight. When that gain touched forty pounds I resumed smoking for a few years, after a two-year lapse into virtue. Cranking the old truck added strength and stamina. By spring I could sow a sixteen-acre hayfield by hand with a "seed fiddler" in just one day. Tossing hay bales and grain sacks put me in trim for the vast quantities of digging and stone carrying involved later in the building of the new house.

By the spring of 1943 I was feeling so exuberantly confident of my farming abilities that we added more cows, and I was milking, by hand, about fifty quarts a day. The government urged increased farm production as a patriotic duty—and provided a butterfat subsidy as a sweetener. Uncle Sam lent me the money to buy the added cows. It was spring, glorious spring in open country. I found I could round up the cows from the pasture in the morning on my bicycle, shouting old hymns at the top of my lungs as I rode along, and tracking the cows to their woodsy hideouts by the dark footprints they left in the dewy grass.

Those exhilarating morning jaunts, and the solid satisfactions of accomplishment, were strenuous fun, but they nourished a fatal flaw: the tendency to take on too much work. I had to get up before five every morning, and finished the last of my chores just before ten each night. On more than one occasion I found myself simply falling asleep at the office typewriter. I rapidly got rid of all the cows except the two low-producing ones for which the children had developed an attachment, and I later disposed of some eighteen young pigs which we were raising on the side. I had learned—at least with cash profit and enjoyment—just how much I could handle in the way of animals and still do justice to my primary job at the newspaper.

At any period other than wartime I perhaps would have run into difficulties with the boss; but for the moment, good reporters who could also sit in as city editor or in other spots were simply unobtainable, and the paper realized this even more keenly than I did. During our first winter the cranky old truck flatly refused to start at anything near zero temperatures. For a grisly two weeks soon after Christmas, while the truck was out of commission, my shared rides with neighbors were also unavailable, and I legged it the three miles to the suburban village of Middleton in zero or colder weather, catching a bus there or thumbing a ride. Often I arrived more than an hour late, but the managing editor merely greeted me with a forced and wintry smile, saying, "Well, try and get here as early as you can." William T. Evjue, the irascible owner-publisher of the *Capital Times,* put it with more minatory acerbity: "Jacobs, you're going to have to make up your mind one of these days whether you are going to be a newspaper reporter or a farmer."

12.

A House
That Scared Us

During that rugged winter of 1942-43, and the next one, Wright stayed at Taliesin instead of making his usual migration to Arizona. But Taliesin had become a lonely place. Several of the apprentices had already left, or were being drafted into the army. Wright was seventy-six years old, still bursting with his usual energy, his mind undoubtedly full of exciting new architectural possibilities. The spurt of activity which started with our first house, its Usonian followers, the Johnson building, and Fallingwater, had re-established his name and preeminence, after the dreadful vacuum of the twenties and the Depression. But the dozens of skilled draftsmen and apprentices, the hands which carried out his plans, were scattered to the four winds. Money was running out, and daily news of a war that he detested must have been a further aggravation. Nevertheless he remained full of his usual bouncy optimism. I wrote him early in spring (one of the few letters of which I did not keep a copy), asking him formally to start thinking about our new house, and urging him to inspect that hilltop site. He replied on April 8, 1943, which happened to be my fortieth birthday:

"Dear Herbert: It's good, and a good sign, to have you back in the fold again! We'll do something worthwhile. And you will start ahead of where you left off. So will we. . . .

"Meanwhile I wish you and Katherine would come up. We will sit down to the affair with what experience we have had, together, as background for a farmhouse with 'what it takes.'

"Give my love to Katherine and the babes."

(Copyright © The Frank Lloyd Wright Foundation 1978)

A postscript added: "I want you to read the *Autobiography*." I presume he was referring to the new section he was adding, covering the years since 1932, a few pages of which I had seen when he drove us out to Taliesin the previous October.

In the next few months we were at Taliesin several times, and again experienced the thrill of anticipation of great things to come which Wright seemed able to evoke and even increase. This time he had a special plum to entice us with—a radically new construction method that could save us a lot of money, he said. Always seeking new ways in which the machine could be utilized to lower housing costs, Wright had conceived a one-step wall which would be even simpler than the "sandwich" wall of three thicknesses of boards used in our first house. He had asked a large manufacturer of fiberboard to develop a synthetic plank about three inches thick and a foot wide, that could serve as both interior and exterior surface, and be insulation as well. It would be laid up in one simple operation, between connecting joints. Wright had designed the house to use such planks and he had proposed that the company furnish them without cost to us, as ours was to be the first house built with them. After all, we were willing experimenters. There was only one catch: he wanted the company to pay Taliesin one hundred thousands dollars for the idea. Our hopes rode high while Wright carried on the negotiations with the giant firm, but in its final answer the company balked at paying Wright any such sum.

Always pressed for money because of the two large Taliesin establishments, in Wisconsin and Arizona, which were supported largely by his architectural fees, Wright still made no complaint to us about the turn-down. Instead he promptly suggested that we could build very nearly the same type of building ourselves, doing the work in our spare time. Using large planks as forms, we could lay up masonry walls a plank's width at a time, on horizontal lines, and place big and colorful flat stones here and there in the exposed face of the concrete. He called this style "desert masonry," and had used it in construction of the buildings at Taliesin West. But he still had no plan on paper to show us.

Perhaps as a sop to our impatience, Wright stopped at the farmhouse in July, 1943, and walked over the fields to choose a site for the new house. He picked a spot near the top of the long slope of field across the road from the farmhouse where a nearby oak woods would be a background, and with a view which swept the fields for miles in all directions.

The scene could scarcely have been more idyllic. Mrs. Wright had come too, and we walked through the field and up the long

Dear Herbert: It's good, and a good sign, to have you back in the fold again!   We'll do something worthwhile. And you will start ahead of where you left off.   So will we.

I'll drop in and see the hill again - soon.

Meantime I wish you and Catherine would come up, and we will sit down to the affair with what experience we have had, together, as background for a farmhouse with "what it takes".

Give my love to Katherind and the babes.

Affection,

Frank Lloyd Wright
TALIESIN: SPRING GREEN: WISCONSIN   April 8th, 1943

I want you to read the Autobiography -

slope over a white carpet of alsike-clover blossoms, close to the ground and soft under our feet as we crushed their white crowns. Wright, with his usual sense of the dramatic, managed to invest the scene with dignity and beauty. His cane waved in the air as he marched to and fro across the clover. "It's just as if he was making music with his cane," Susan whispered. He finally chose a spot, and pointed his cane to the ground. "We'll have the barn, a small one, back there, down the slope, and here, all before you—this," and the cane swept toward the horizon three miles away. We seemed to be at the center of concentric circles.

We had envisioned, and suggested to Wright, a location at the extreme north end of the field, where the land was even higher and commanded a view over Lake Mendota, three miles away, and the hills as far as fifteen miles distant, but Wright would have none of it. "You never can tell what the highway department will do," he said, warning that they might slash down most of the rather steep hillside for a road-widening and grading. And he added, "Never build on top of your best view. Build near it, and walk to it, and you'll appreciate it more." His own Taliesin had been built curving around the brow of a hill, not on top.

Wright proved prophetic about the highway department. It later marked the road for a drastic widening which would have been devastating to any house placed where we thought it should be. Even without the widening, postwar traffic increased enormously, creating a noisy location. However, we did welcome his suggestion of "a place to walk to," and I built a rough picnic table and benches which we used often, during and after the war.

As we thought about the do-it-yourself construction that Wright urged, we may have had a few qualms about our ability to handle that much in the way of concrete construction, but nothing could stand long against Wright's magic persuasive powers. We had already survived almost a year of fairly rugged farm life, and thought we were rather able. The picture we had in mind, as we kept pressing Wright for a drawing of what it would look like, was of something along the lines of the first house.

With 1943 our first summer on the farm, we became absorbed in that life and reconciled to the idea that the war would last at least another year (we could not visualize two years yet). We thought there might be a little delay afterwards, maybe as much as six months, before we would be able to move into a spanking new house, with indoor plumbing, fireplace, and splendid views framed by the best of architecture. The actual five years that it did take would have seemed wildly punitive.

And yet life was becoming more pleasant. The most heartening acquisition that summer was a middle-aged Ford convertible with a ragged top, to replace the decrepit old bakery truck. Thanks to its fairly new tires, and the general scarcity of any vehicle, we sold the quondam bread wagon for twice what we had paid for it, and went careering about the countryside, top down, children shouting and parents beaming their solid satisfaction.

Another great pleasure was a garden big enough at last to fulfill all our desires. We devoted the rich soil of a corner of a field near the house to nearly an acre of garden, where I made room for things like celery, melons, gourds, and many root crops like potatoes that we could store for the winter. For the first time we were going to have sweet corn practically running out of our ears. I made several plantings, a big early one to catch the high-priced first-of-season market, and later small ones to keep our own table going until frost. About the time the garden was beginning to flourish and need attention I had got rid of most of the cows, so chores were comparatively light.

Katherine and I found special pleasure in rising early and going out into the cornfield heavy with fragrance and dew, just as the sun was coming up, to bag about twenty dozen ears of corn that I would drop off at a grocery near the office. We were aware that the sugar in sweet corn changes to starches within a few hours of picking, and for our own use followed the practice of "having the water boiling before you start to pick." That's why most city dwellers have never tasted real sweet corn. But I got a shock when I dumped my corn into the grocer's bin, explained that it had just been picked, and asked him if he wanted another load the next day. "Oh no," said he, "that'll last us three days. I still have some left from last time." The grocer had probably never tasted real corn either, but in spite of his indifference we continued to enjoy picking in the early morning, rather than the night before as most truck farmers did.

Well before that first spring on the farm, while the snows of winter still pressed around us, the children—and their parents—got a special thrill with the arrival of the first lambs. We had acquired four ewes from an old professor friend. The first

Replacing the balky old bakery truck, the Ford convertible was a constant delight for the whole family, and with a two-wheel trailer hauled feed, calves, pigs, an occasional steer—and, later, building materials for the new house. (Photo by Herbert Jacobs)

lamb that arrived, on a cold mid-February day, was a beauty: covered with warm curly white wool, and adorable. The children were fascinated and returned often to the barn to sit in the straw in the corner of the boxstall and watch as the wobbly little lamb explored its new world in hunger and curiosity.

Later that spring Katherine's father sent from New Jersey twin purebred Suffolk lambs, which we promptly named Romeo and Juliet. With their black heads and long legs they were a striking pair, and became the foundation for our flock. The enthusiastic Romeo became so domineering the second year that I had to stake him out in the farmyard, and described him, to the amusement of our city friends, as our ball-bearing lawnmower.

Early that spring we had moved to a sort of pinnacle among the neighboring farmers (although they would always consider us amateur bunglers at farming) by building a hotbed from which we furnished tomato, pepper and other plants to the farm wives for

Me, giving a ration of oats to my favorite Suffolk ram, Romeo.
(Photo by Edgar Tafel)

their gardens. Farmers, of course, spent all their energy getting the major crops into the soil, and the spring work had to be completed before the farm wife could even get the garden plowed. A luxury like a hotbed was unheard of around there, and our gifts of plants raised us mightily in the regard of the farm wives, and even earned a bit of grudging respect from their husbands.

Possibly from force of habit we jogged Wright from time to time, by letter or in person, to produce a plan for the house that he had promised, but nothing happened until December. This was his second successive winter in Wisconsin, and Taliesin had become a much smaller circle. Clients were now as scarce as apprentices. Wright had time at last to put our dream house on paper. With two dear friends who were visiting, we hurried out on December 2, 1943, in response to the master's call that he had something to show.

Once again came that magic moment when everything seemed to be just what we wanted, and Wright was at his most charming and persuasive to explain it all. We saw a floor plan and a perspective drawing of a rather large square-shaped living room area, two stories high, and a low bedroom wing extending out from it, with a bath and a powder room, two small bedrooms, and a large master bedroom with its own fireplace. What luxury! The enormous living room also had a mezzanine across one end. In the opposite direction from the bedroom wing, a roofed passageway led to a small barn with room for a horse, a couple of cows or steers, and some sheep. It was, in fact, a fitting estate for a country gentleman and his wife and family. The way Wright presented it, with all those economies and the understanding that we would be doing most of the building ourselves, it all seemed possible and ideal. We left, trailing clouds of glory. However, my Garden Book, for once perversely laconic, merely reported in an entry that night that we had gone out to Taliesin that day and seen plans for the new house.

Doubts had begun to creep in even before we reached the farmhouse. Where was the simple life we had enjoyed in the first house? And what had become of Wright's promise of "another $5,000 house?" Well into our second winter on the farm, we also wondered what the cold southwest winds would do to our heating bills. At bottom stemmed a basic difference in financial philosophies between us and Wright. Partly because of the nature

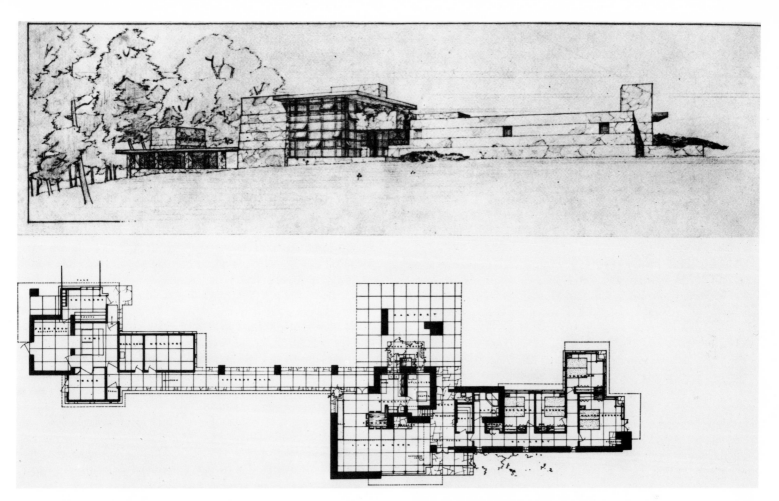

Wright showed us a perspective and floor plan similar to this one in December, 1943, saying we could do much of the construction ourselves, but we decided that it was more elaborate than we felt suited us and that it did not invite the informal way of life we had learned to love in the first house. Though accepted by two later clients, the house was never built. (First published in *Architectural Forum*, Jan. 1948, © Time, Inc.)

of his work, partly from his way of life, he was not afraid to run up bills and trust to the future to provide the money somehow. "So long as we had the luxuries, the necessities could pretty well take care of themselves," he said of the early years of his marriage and children, and he enthusiastically carried out that philosophy all his life. Katherine and I, on the contrary, had been raised in families that practiced rigid economy, families that could not even conceive of going into debt for a *luxury*. And we still carried that horror of going into debt.

These three letters resulted from our long hours of discussion:

Tuesday, Dec. 7, 1943

"Dear Mr. Wright: When I got home from the office Friday with the draft of a letter I proposed to send you, Katherine pulled out one of her own.

"I have copied them, and here they are, and may you read them with an understanding eye.

"As always, our visit at Taliesin Thursday was a tremendous pleasure, and we thank you again on our guests' behalf as well as our own. —H.J."

The two separate letters we had composed were dated December 3, the day after our visit, but we did not send them immediately. We talked it all over, thought of various kinds of joint letters, but decided to stick to our original versions. I did not apparently keep copies of the letters, but the Taliesin archives furnished copies to me. Katherine thinks she wrote more, and the single page does not in fact contain a signature, but Taliesin was unable to locate any more pages. Here is my letter:

Friday, Dec. 3, 1943

"Dear Mr. Wright: That was a wonderful house you showed us, and surely you were a most enchanting advocate, but we are agreed, on later thought, that it is not for us.

"It is hard to put into words just why it is not for us, but much of it goes back to our experience with the Westmorland house: Neither Katherine nor I wish to be in the position again of carrying a heavy financial load (in proportion to our income, of course) to pay off on a house, and also to heat it. And because of all that to run the risk of losing it.

"For one thing, we are not talking the same language when we talk about a $10,000 house. You are thinking of the shell, which probably could be put up for $10,000. And I am thinking of the thing I would be moving into, which means shell plus floor coverings, plus furniture, plus storm windows, aeroshades, stove, refrigerator, washing machine, etc., which means two or three thousand more. Of course these are not properly part of the cost of construction, but they must be paid for just the same. Off hand, I can't think of anybody, least of all myself, who is worth a $12,000 house.

"What we wanted—still do, for that matter—was something considerably smaller and less costly, and without great spaces to be heated during the winter. You remember we suggested a sort of "inner core" to which we could retire in the snowy season. When we got home from Taliesin we talked for several hours of what might be done, such as making the bedrooms and living room smaller, cutting out powder room and mezzanine, etc., but I'm afraid these would all be things that would end in something inharmonious in design.

"It isn't that we don't love your houses. We do. So much so that we would rather not break our backs to pay for living in them, or, especially, risk the chance of losing one again.

"I am enclosing the Chicago interview clipping of which I spoke.

My warmest regards to you."

Katherine's letter strikes much the same note:

"Dear Mr. Wright: You are probably the world's greatest salesman. Your client's mind becomes a complete and lovely blank as her eye follows the line of a snow-capped roof on the beautiful house. You had better sell it to the Silo Company—a good profit making institution which can afford its luxury.

"Perhaps it would be better to start over because I know one cannot make many changes and maintain the integrity of a building. When we got home and tried to live in the house we realized there were several things that we had spoken of before which were "musts" which were not in this drawing.

"First is the general cost of the building—it must be at least a third less. We know of course that would demand a sacrifice in space and luxury of design, rather than in quality of construction. We must not make the mistake of assuming such a big financial burden in a house, that we have no energy or money left to enjoy the life a fine home could offer.

"Second, there must not be any costly heating problems such as 13 ft. ceilings and mezzanines, as attractive and livable as they may be. We shall probably never have more income than we have now and a big fuel bill each year can take the extras out of a small salary, such as music for the children, etc. This second point would also seem to specify the use of coal rather than oil. This would mean a separate furnace room, perhaps underground, below a service room.

"The third is only a matter of arrangement of rooms in relationship to the duo-life we do and would live. With the combination of school and office clothes, plus farm functions, the entrance to the house from the barn should be to the service room where the rough and dirty clothes can be kept. The service room should be accessible to the kitchen so that the milk utensils, large vegetable pickings, etc. can be handled in the service room. Unless this is well co-ordinated the dirt and disorder of the farm can destroy the charm of the rest of the house and make more work for me than I can do. Perhaps the kitchen should be less open to the dining and living room, because with a family in the country it is less orderly.

"The two items in the construction which are so attractive, namely the stone construction and the window design, can serve as well in a smaller house."

Wright took a few days before replying, and when he did answer he was his usual sympathetic—and provocative—self:

"Dear Herb and Katherine: I think you are both almost right. Trouble is, every time I've tried to economize it cost me so much more than it was worth that I was forced to abandon it and go natural. There is always what is called the economic limit—meaning the limits within which "economy" really economizes.

"You ought to know (or will after you have tried it for long enough) what those limits are for you. I am, after all, only your architect—not your banker or your sky pilot.

"So I shall be guided strictly by your own consciences in this

matter, not by mine. Like Festus Jones, I fear what little I have altogether is guilty by now.

"We'll try to co-operate with you and let you burst your bonds as the chrysalis does . . . in due season as you may.

"However, I do not like your assumption that your "income" (if that is what you insist upon calling the thing) "is never going to be more than it is." I have more faith in the country than that, although it is getting a worm's eye view of itself right now. That assumption of yours is always stultifying and it is fascism, too, — old country stuff — you know?

"Every true Democrat is a gambler with Fate and Circumstance. And loves it."

Wright himself had corrected the letter (doubtless typed by Eugene Masselink, his secretary), capitalizing Fate and Circumstance. He proved correct about my income, which at that time was frozen under wartime regulations. In the spring of 1948 I took on extra work as a part-time teacher in the University of Wisconsin School of Journalism, and also began a daily newspaper column, which I wrote at home, and for which I was paid extra. I continued both activities during my fourteen remaining years with the *Capital Times,* and they soon brought in nearly as much money as my regular newspaper salary—which advanced too. I also made a small amount of money writing books and articles. The inflation of land values after the war produced added income. Selling the old house and barn at inflated post-war prices went a long way toward paying for the new house.

Wright had indicated that if we did not accept the plan of the house he would probably offer it to M.N. Hein, of Chippewa Falls, Wisconsin, an officer of the Madison Silo Company, which had a branch in Chippewa Falls. Hein's partner, Clyde Woody, was the absentee owner of the farm we had bought. The farm had one of the company's silos, plus a lot of concrete silo staves used for walks, tanks and other construction. Wright modified the design of the barn, and added a study to the house design, for Hein. Although the house advanced to working drawings, Hein died at that time and it was never constructed. Wright used the same basic plan again in the proposed Bloomfield house planned for Arizona, which also was never built.

Responding to long letters from Katherine and me rejecting his design for a new house in the country as too costly, Wright told us to ignore fears that our income might not increase. (Copyright © The Frank Lloyd Wright Foundation 1978)

Dear Herb and Katherine:

I think you are both almost right. Trouble is, every time I've tried to economize it cost me so much more than it was worth that I was forced to abandon it and go natural. There is always, what is called, the economic limit – meaning the limits within which "economy" really economizes.

You ought to know (or will after you have tried it for long enough) what those limits are for you. I am, after all, only your architect – not your banker or your sky-pilot.

So I shall be guided strictly by your own consciences in this matter, not by mine. Like Festus Jones, I fear what little I have altogether is guilty by now.

We'll try to cooperate with you and let you burst your bonds as the crysalis does . . . in due season as you may.

However, I do not like your assumption that your "income" (if that is what you insist upon calling the thing) "is never going to be more than it is". I have more faith in the country than that, although it is getting a wormseye view of itself right now. That assumption of yours is always stultifying and it is fascism, too, – old country stuff – you know?

Every true Democrat is a gambler with Fate and Circumstance. And loves it.

Faithfully,
Frank Lloyd Wright
December 11th, 1943

80

13.

The Solar Windtrap

Wright's commission about this time to design a museum in New York City to house the Solomon R. Guggenheim collection of non-representational art undoubtedly changed our own future when it led Wright into thinking in terms of circular patterns.

In his early life he had left his mark on Chicago in his work under Louis Sullivan on the Auditorium theater and hotel, and through the enormous push he gave to the development of modern architecture with his designs for dwellings in the Chicago area. But New York, the biggest prize, had eluded him. What could he do in his productive old age—he was then seventy-seven—that would truly astound this blasé metropolis?

Wright loved this sort of situation: plenty of money, a broad-minded client, an eye-catching site on Fifth Avenue near the Metropolitan Museum, and a city that might rise, bristling, to his challenge. Wright reached back into the rich storehouse of his past for an idea that could be modified or transformed for a new site and purpose. Whether it was done subconsciously or deliberately, the Guggenheim Museum, with its upward and outward sweeping spiral, was a mirror image of a project for a circular tower that narrowed as it reached upward, and had been intended to house a planetarium. Spurred by Guggenheim and the Baroness Hilla Rebay, Guggenheim's mentor on non-representational art, Wright must have been pondering the Guggenheim design through much of 1943.

The situation also held a curious parallel to our first house. At that time, in 1936, Wright had just received the commission for the Johnson administration building, not long before we came to him. With our first house he was interested in trying out the floor heating system which he intended to use in both the Johnson administration building and the elaborate home for the Johnsons.

(Herbert Johnson sat on a stool in our kitchen in order to see the new type of heating in action before his own installation was completed.) Wright had reached back into his experiences in the Orient to recall the Korean-type floor heating which he translated into steam pipes for our house.

The combination of the Guggenheim requirements and our own much more modest needs may well have provided some stimulating cross-fertilization as he meditated the solar house. One of the major requirements we had stressed was some way of checkmating the chilling southwest winds of winter, which we had got a taste of in the first house, experienced more strongly in the exposed farmhouse, and begun to be seriously alarmed about for that highly exposed hilltop. Once again Wright drew on his past experience for an answer, but its birth was tantalizingly slow as far as we were concerned. The first stirrings came in a brief note from Wright dated December 30, 1943. He wrote:

"We are at work on a more simple scheme, as you propose. We hope it will be ready soon!"

Immersed as we were in the rich new experience of farm life, and with a new baby in the house to center our attention, we were not nearly so impatient as we had been for the Usonian house. The war dragged on and we knew it would be years before the reality of a house appeared. Nevertheless, there was a certain puckish quality about Wright that showed itself often, and it appeared in his next letter. After an interval, which must have been largely devoted to the Guggenheim, he wrote, on February 8, 1944:

"Dear Herb Jacobs: We are about ready to make you 'the goat' for a fresh enterprise in architecture. If you don't get what is on the boards some other fellow will. So 'watch out.' It's *good*.

"I think we have a real 'first' that you will like a lot.

"Only the 'picture' remains to be done — suppose you come out next Sunday. FLLW."

Wright had added in pencil the quotation marks around "the goat" and "first," and had added the sentences "So 'watch out.' It's *good*."

Astoundingly, considering our consuming interest in the topic, I did not put down a single word in the Garden Book about the

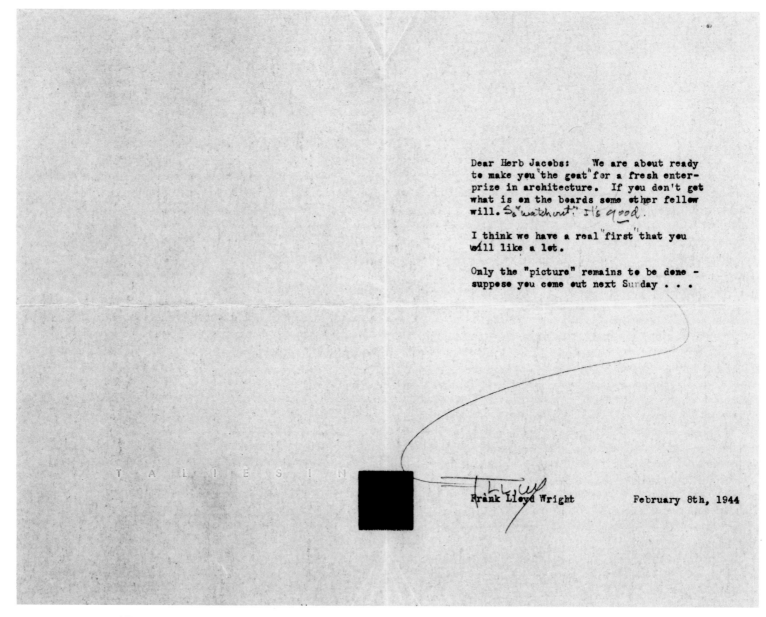

Dear Herb Jacobs: We are about ready
to make you "the goat" for a fresh enter-
prize in architecture. If you don't get
what is on the boards some other fellow
will. So "watch out." It's good.

I think we have a real "first" that you
will like a lot.

Only the "picture" remains to be done -
suppose you come out next Sunday . . .

Frank Lloyd Wright   February 8th, 1944

His newest plan is a ''real first,'' Wright says, inviting us to come and look. The design was for the solar hemicycle which we began to build some two years later. (Copyright © The Frank Lloyd Wright Foundation 1978)

letters, or about the subsequent visit to look at what would be the third house that Wright designed for us, after we had rejected the second house.

But of course we were very curious when we were invited to Taliesin Sunday, February 13, 1944, to see what the architect had in store for us in the promised new venture in architecture that he held as tempting bait in his letter. We were ushered into the old drafting room, but Wright put us off at first when we asked excitedly to see the "picture" of the new house. He left us in the drafting room for some reason, and when he did not come back immediately, we peeked into the adjoining room. There, on the walls, we glimpsed no less than eight colored sketches of what we took to be our house, together with some smaller colored sketches which we learned later were of the proposed Guggenheim museum.

When Wright finally returned we made no sign that we had seen the sketches, which had been incomprehensible anyway without explanation. With what we took to be hesitation and uncertainty—he had written in his autobiography that the first presentation of plans to a client was always a difficult moment—he led us to the sketches, and began explaining them.

Reminding us that we had been concerned about the cold southwest winds of winter, Wright pointed to the semi-circular shape of the house, which faced a half-circle of garden sunk some four feet below floor level—the floor level itself being a foot and a half below grade level. Facing the sunken garden, behind a narrow terrace, a solid band of glass doors and windows, forty-eight feet long, rose fourteen feet to the overhanging roof. Behind the house, at the north side of the structure, a slope of dirt reached almost to the narrow band of windows, about a foot high, which circled the entire rear of the house.

With the big windows at the front, the low-lying winter sun would come way into the house and help to warm it, but the high summer sun would be cut off by the roof overhang, Wright said. The other feature to counter the cold weather, he declared, was the creation of an airfoil by streamlining in place. "The sunken garden in front of the hemicycle acts to form a ball of dead air, and the long slope of dirt against the back wall is necessary so that the wind will blow over the house instead of against it," Wright said. "When it is finished, you can stand on your front terrace in a strong wind and light your pipe without any trouble. With little wind blowing against it, and with the mass of dirt at your back, your heating costs will be very low."

Wright said that he had used the same system some fifty years earlier, when he had been asked by Madison park authorities to design a boat house and shed for one of the Madison lakes, the chief architectural problem being to provide a quiet, virtually windless mooring shelter which would still have its open side to the lake. The structure was in fact built, and Wright said that the airfoil principle had worked perfectly, though the building was later torn down. Wright recalled with a smile that the pipe-lighting ceremony was performed when the boathouse was completed, and properly amazed the participants. He declared, however, that this "streamlining in place" principle had never before been applied to houses.

"You're getting another 'first,' " Wright said. "Here is the answer to the problem of what to build on a hilltop exposed to the full sweep of the wind. In fact, it is suitable for almost any spot in the country where there is good drainage, for the house creates its own site and its own view."

Bit by bit we absorbed other details. The plan provided for no less than five bedrooms, all on a mezzanine or balcony a few feet back of the big windows at the front. This would give us a double-height living room, running the full length of the house, with the kitchen at one end, and a fireplace in the back wall, near the center. A large circular tower, rising a few feet above the level of the roof, straddled the back wall. Wright explained that it would contain the utilities, a staircase to the mezzanine, and a big bathroom on the mezzanine.

Wright called attention to a large circle bisecting the row of windows at the front, and said it would contain a pool for plants and fish, half inside and half outside the line of windows. To make a good story, we should have shouted at that moment, "That can be the plunge pool we have wanted ever since we tried the one at Fallingwater," but the thought did not immediately occur to us. It did soon afterward, however, and we carried it out.

The architect capped our joy for that day by assuring us that he thought the house could indeed be built for five thousand dollars, which promptly banished any small doubts and fears which we might have harbored. With that kind of price tag, especially since

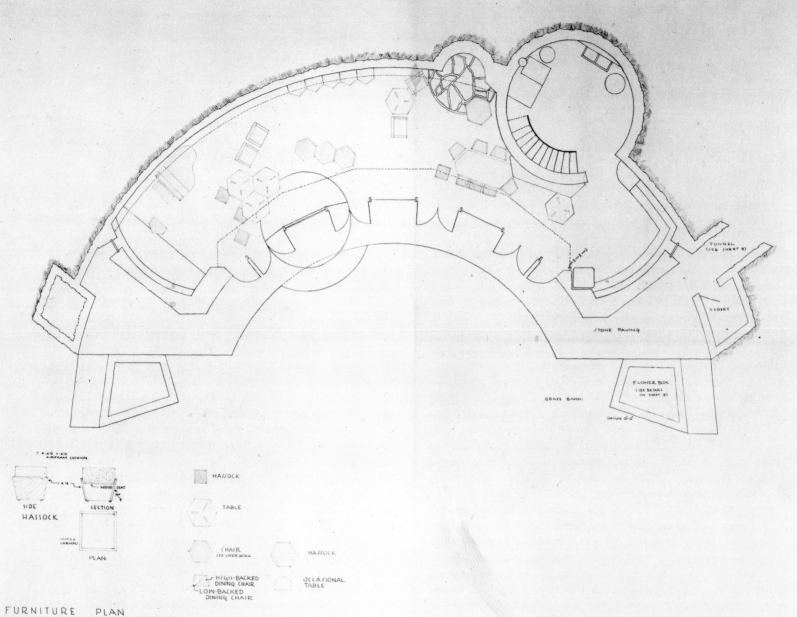

TUNNEL
(SEE SHEET 3)

STONE PAVING

CLOSET

FLOWER BOX
(SEE DETAILS
ON SHEET 3)

GRASS BANK

DATUM 0'-0"

7 x 16'5 x 16'5
AIRFOAM CUSHION

1 x 12

WOOD SEAT

SIDE   SECTION
HASSOCK

MITRE
CORNERS

PLAN

HASSOCK

TABLE

CHAIR
SEE LATER DETAIL

HASSOCK

HIGH-BACKED
DINING CHAIR

OCCASIONAL
TABLE

LOW-BACKED
DINING CHAIR

FURNITURE PLAN

HOUSE FOR MR AND MRS HERBERT JACOBS   MIDDLETON, WISCONSIN

FRANK   LLOYD   WRIGHT   ARCHITECT

Wright provided this furniture layout, which is almost identical with the floor plan of the solar hemicycle. The module of the house was a six-degree sector of a circle, measured from a post in the center of the sunken garden. Thus the mullions of doors and windows at the front were two sectors apart, the fireplace measured two sectors, the utility room circle was four sectors in diameter, and so forth, enabling the whole house to be laid out with a transit and steel tape. Including the outer points of the end flower boxes, the house formed a virtual half circle, facing the half circle of the sunken garden. Later drawings gave details of open shelves and furniture layouts for the bedrooms. (Copyright © The Frank Lloyd Wright Foundation, 1978)

he had already done it for us once before at that price, we did not even blanch at the imposing size of the house, or even think that a sixty-foot living room might seem a trifle big.

We clamored for a drawing to take home with us, but Wright gently refused. "If you took a drawing home, you'd be showing it around and then somebody would steal this idea," he said. "I'd like to get at least this one house built before it is copied." We had to be content with that—but of course I tried to draw my own design at home from memory, with only partial success. What a house to stir our imaginations for the next months!

Wright showed us the color renderings of the house from various perspectives. (Incidentally, we never saw them again.) He took equal delight in giving us a look at the small color drawings of the Guggenheim museum. I believe we were the first persons outside of Taliesin who saw them, for they had been executed only a few days before, he said.

In the first set of solar house plans, Wright's design showed a "butterfly roof," draining at the center crease into four-inch pipes which also supported the mezzanine at about twelve-foot intervals. In the second set of plans Wright fortunately removed the pipe-posts from the living room floor, and hung the mezzanine on rods from the rafters, masking the rods inside the corners of the bedroom partitions. The now-flat roof was slightly tilted toward the rear of the house for drainage.

When it came time to build, we liked and used the new design for the mezzanine and roof, but in the second set of plans Wright had also changed the design for the forty-eight feet of glass doors and windows at the front. Instead of a wooden plate at nine feet, with fixed glass above, he now called for doors and windows which would each be a solid sheet of glass fourteen feet high. We thought they would be expensive and unmanageable, and so we used the first set of plans for the windows, with the plate at nine feet.

Most surprising to us, Wright had also changed the design of the pool in the second set of plans from straight-sided, with a concrete divider between inside and outside pools, to a dish-shaped affair with sloping sides and a glass partition. The window mullions came down into the water in copper boots. But we wanted a plunge pool, so we used the first set of plans, with the mullions resting on a concrete divider. (In his very first sketch, Wright had shown the pool at sixteen feet in diameter, instead of the later twelve feet, and had placed it in the center of the windows.)

Later Wright had the apprentices build an elaborate model of the Guggenheim, after the plans had gone through the inevitable modification and refinement as new ideas came to him. The model was hinged at one side, so that it could be swung open to show the interior ramp. We happened to be at Taliesin when he came back from a shopping tour in Madison that summer, happy as a child with a new toy as he poured out strings of dime store beads, which he draped over balconies and parapets to simulate vines. Another device he used was small segments of macaroni, painted and strung together, or bunched, to represent trailing vines or flowers. They relieved the starkness of the model when it was photographed for magazine and newspaper reproduction.

Besides our house and the Guggenheim, 1944 and the next year saw several other projects on the drawing boards based on the circular theme. The Morris store in San Francisco, built inside an old warehouse, had a curving ramp reminiscent of the Guggenheim. The Huntington Hartford project for a hotel and sports club, and the Daphne funeral parlor in San Francisco, were two others. Wright was entranced by the mysteries of the undertaking business, and highly amused when he learned that the basement entrance for bodies and coffins was described as "that's where the merchandise is brought in."

The solar hemicycle as it appeared nearly two years after construction. In the foreground is the sunken garden, with the bulge of stonework for the outside pool, and the "elephant ear" aquatic plants of the inside pool pressing against the glass. Elizabeth and William, leaning against a fraction of the forty-eight feet of doors and windows, show the scale of the house. Outdoor planting is not completed, and the flower boxes, waiting for junipers to grow, are decorated with cut pine boughs. (Photo © Ezra Stoller)

14.

The Slow Beginning

Wright had spent most of the winter in Wisconsin, but the growing establishment at Taliesin West, near Scottsdale, Arizona, lured him more and more as the winter dragged on. A month after we had seen the drawings of the solar house Wright sent one of his short notes, opening with a variant of the classic sentence employed to teach neophyte reporters how to type, which goes, "Now is the time for all good men to come to the aid of the party."

He said that we could send two hundred and fifty dollars "on account," and added that plans were nearly done. The reason for the demand for money was because they were going west for a few weeks, the letter continued. It was dated March 21, 1944. A hand correction on the typed letter softened the demand for money by ending it with Wright's favorite device of a question mark.

For a change he caught me feeling affluent. I had had more than a year free of monthly mortgage payments, and the sale of some acres of the farmland that I did not plan to use had cleared my farm indebtedness. Our living expenses were lower because we were getting so much from the land and livestock. I wrote him, still cautiously refraining from exhibiting any great wealth:

"Delighted to know that plans are almost ready—also that you are going to be able to get away for a little needed rest.

"Being temporarily flush, I hurry to oblige with the Guggenheim touch. I assume that the enclosed payment of $250 is on account on a 10% fee basis, figuring the house at $5,500 or less, which is the building cost you mentioned.

"The question we are palpitating to know is whether we get a 'picture' to look at besides what I drew from memory with a home-made compass the night we got home from Taliesin. We promise not to show it around.

"Well anyway—bon voyage and bless you all."

I got an acknowledgement from his secretary for the money, and an assertion that plans and specifications were going forward. Perhaps they were, but the progress was glacial. For nearly two years I pleaded, begged, cajoled in ceaseless efforts to get my hands on those "plans and specifications." When the war ended, and a wave of prospective clients swept toward Taliesin, many of them clutching fistfuls of money that I could not hope to match, or with enticing problems that would attract Wright's attention, I became almost frantic. Wright knew better than I did, of course, that there really was no hurry. Building materials were still under strict wartime priorities, and likely to remain so.

Vast projects already engrossed his attention. One was the proposed Rogers Lacy Hotel in Dallas, Texas, and Wright boasted to me that it represented "my first million-dollar fee." Another was the battle of titans shaping up between Wright and Robert Moses, the energetic New York official who wore so many administrative hats that he was a walking hat rack. Moses later made rumbling noises that demanded changes which would block building of the Guggenheim Museum. Eventually the battle, carried on largely through the newspapers, ended with Wright making a few minor changes, and both monumental egos claiming a victory.

We continued to receive bulletins from the Taliesin front, including a strictly down-to-earth one from William Wesley Peters, the young architect who had married Svetlana, Mrs. Wright's daughter by a former marriage. His cheerful letter, dated April 8, 1944, made it sound as if plans would soon be in our hands.

Peters said work on the drawings was progressing very satisfactorily, and declared that Wright had virtually completed his own work on the drawings for the house. He himself was writing to find out just what we wanted in the way of livestock space in the little barn, so that he could start laying it out on the drafting board. He said the layout they had contemplated provided for two cows, two horses, and space for as many as thirty chickens. He even wanted to know whether we intended to raise calves for veal, and if so whether we would need separate pen space. Also, did we intend to keep any hogs or other animals? Peters himself would soon have a large beef cattle farm on land near Taliesin And as to the prospective drawing of the house which we had asked for, Peters said it would be forthcoming as soon as possible.

I sent our list of requirements back to Peters. I believe we substituted sheep pens for horses, and did not provide for either pigs or chickens, as we felt that so many varieties of animals in the same close quarters would not be compatible. And that was the last we saw of any barn plan or proposal. Something similar to it appears, connected to the house by a covered walkway, in the drawing for the Hein house (intended for Chippewa Falls, Wisconsin), which was a modification of the plan we had rejected in December, 1943. For the Hein house Wright added a photographic darkroom and a workshop, two items which I did not request.

For the next two years, after the brave start of the spring of 1944 on plans, we sat—but not in silence—and made occasional visits to Taliesin. I continued to pepper Wright with cheery notes asking how the plans were coming, and urging him to take another look at the site now that he was planning a radically different design. Toward the end of the two years I tried to stir his interest in some nearby stone quarries.

Wright answered my fervent pleas with a series of masterly one-liners. Each letter, consisting of a single line, expressed variations on the theme that he would be over to see us as soon as he could find the time, and that he greeted us affectionately. What he did not do was come—and with so many much larger projects turning over in his mind there was really no good reason why he should.

In the spring of 1945, to mark the end of a long winter, we built our first large easy chair for the new house, patterning it, from memory, on the two large easy chairs which the Wescott cousins had made for our first house. I had no power tools, but was able to cut the miters satisfactorily with a handsaw. Katherine did the upholstery so expertly that the job appeared to be practically professional. There was scarcely room for the chair in the small farmhouse living room, which was already congested with a piano, an oil stove heater, a giant overstuffed rocker bought at a farm auction for three dollars, and a table and long bench which I had built in. By that time son William was agile and big enough to leap from piano bench to built-in bench, and thence on to rocker and big easy chair in one dazzling circuit that never touched the floor. We were delighted with his performance, because his orbit now took him out of range of the oil heater; we were always afraid he would knock it over and burn the house down before we had the new one built.

Actually, it was a happy time for us. We were at ease in our farm situation, loving the outdoors and the involvement with farm animals. We admired the independence and self-sufficiency the children had developed. Thanks to the wartime rationing of meat and butter, our city friends found us a special attraction, with our homemade butter, and a freezer stuffed with meat, plus the chance to let their children mingle with docile animals. Neighbors, some of whom lived in mortal terror of paper and pencil, dropped by to have me help them compose want ads—not necessarily for my own paper. I felt honored when the neighbors elected me treasurer of the three-man board of our one-room school. I did learn later that any new man in the community (I use man advisedly: it would not have occurred to anyone even to propose a woman for the board) was promptly talked into being put on the school board. He would find out soon enough what endless petty detail and bickering were part of his annual five-dollar salary.

Many of our city friends, who couldn't at first reconcile themselves to the fact that we had abandoned that lovely Frank Lloyd Wright house in the city, came to envy our new country freedom, but only two ventured to follow our example. Sometimes their children pushed the parents into frankness about it.

"Daddy, why can't we live in the country like the Jacobses?" a little girl asked one Sunday.

"Because your mother doesn't know anything about it, and I haven't got the guts," was her father's brutally frank reply.

Ever since that first summer when Wright had walked over to the hilltop with us and picked out a spot for the new house, I had kept the place marked. Naturally, in a tillable field, I wasn't going to make an island out of it, but with stones and very low stakes I kept the place clearly identifiable, and we refreshed our visions of future splendor by visiting there, enjoying the sense of the landscape "all coming together in that spot." Now and then we wondered whether Wright really had a design that would foil the wind—especially in times of heavy snow, when we could not even get near the hallowed place, but could see it from the farmhouse, the distant field smoking with the constantly blowing snow.

Toward the end of the war, with the children more mature, the Wrights took to inviting them to join us on our trips to Taliesin. Part of Wright's charm lay in his treating children as well as parents as individuals. He knew their names, and sought out any talents they might have. Himself proficient on the piano, he had Susan play for him on Taliesin's magnificent grand piano, listened thoughtfully, and commented, "A bit heavy on the pedal." (A dozen years later, as a member of the Taliesin Fellowship, she became the accompanist for Taliesin's chorus and orchestra.)

Susan, being older than the other two children, had usually accompanied us to Taliesin in the years before the younger ones were invited. On one occasion she calmly seated herself in a large armchair at the front of the circle in front of the fireplace when we all went into the living room for music after dinner. Wright, solicitous for his other guests but still careful to respect the rights of small persons, went over to her and asked if she would like to sit in a smaller chair, or on the floor. Unaware that she was usurping space usually reserved for grownups, Susan merely smiled sweetly but did not move. Wright, still polite but determined, went all the way back to his studio and returned with an attractive leopard skin rug to tempt her, but in vain. Rather than make a disciplinary scene, Katherine told Susan, "Maybe we can both sit in this big chair," and joined her, but Wright's great patience with childhood independence remained long afterward in her memory.

At home the newly built easy chair, which coincided with the end of the war, served as a daily reminder of things to come, spurring us toward a burst of building enthusiasm. With the end of rationing we soon achieved that citified pinnacle of civilization, an inside flush toilet, plus a gas stove to replace the old wood and coal stove, and a gas refrigerator to fill the spot of the old ice box. Both these were purchased with an eye to their place in the new house.

By the spring of 1946 our building temperature stood at fever pitch. Wright was encouraging, almost to the point of producing at long last a set of plans, but stuck to promises instead. Butter and gasoline were off the ration list, but building materials were still tied to a system of federal priorities. I noticed the hubbub over the granting of such a blessing to a controversial race track in California, and saw taverns and similar amenities being approved all around us in Wisconsin. Surely this simple little farmhouse that we proposed to build ought to qualify, especially if I could show that its radical design might well set a new pattern, as the Usonian house had done.

Madison's leading bank was so anxious to lend money that people filling out deposit slips found themselves targets of friendly top-level banker persuaders—it even happened to me. I wrote up a proposal and handed it to the bank May 15, 1946, describing the innovations: the indoor-outdoor pool, the semicircular shape, and the unusual protection from the wind. I even drew them a rough floor plan and perspective from memory.

I doubt if the project horrified them, but they may have been amused at my efforts at persuasion. Details such as the pools, the wild idea of protecting a house from the wind by the application of aerodynamic principles, heating through the floor, and bedrooms on a balcony must have startled them a bit. They did look at the idea, but only from curiosity, and perhaps to show to architect friends for whatever ideas could be lifted. In two weeks they gave a polite but firm no, saying, "The bank does not wish to get involved with anything outside the city limits." The fact that they could have told me so when I applied merely confirmed my suspicions that they were just curious to see what Wright was up to next.

Along with the bank application I painstakingly filled out elaborate forms in triplicate, under the federal Priorities Regulation 33 of the Soil Conservation Service, asking for priorities (actually just a hunting license) for materials for the house. I even appeared before the county and state control boards, whose members listened with straight faces to what I thought were my ingenious pleas, which I followed up by stating to them in a letter:

"1. The experimental design holds great possibilities for Wisconsin and the rest of the country in savings of fuel.

"2. The construction, by elimination of materials critical now and likely to remain so for some years, could stimulate a new type of building which would permit many more houses to be built from the supply of materials likely to be available.

"It goes without saying that it is desirable to build this house now, so that it may be studied and its good features adopted, before the major building boom hits the country."

The only thing I had overlooked was the built-in prejudice in his home area, on the part of all administrators, local, state and federal, against anything that involved Frank Lloyd Wright.

I reported the turndown to Wright in a letter on July 20, 1946, and it promptly rang a bell—a financial one. I wrote that we thought we could go ahead, even without priorities, and added:

"When we talked to you in May, you suggested that it might be a good idea to get a good start this summer and fall, and finish next spring. The more Katherine and I have pondered, the more we felt that we'd like to make a beginning and just push along as best we can. The trouble with waiting until next spring to start is that so much good building weather would be taken up with getting the site ready, well drilling, etc., all of which, and probably some masonry, could be done this summer and fall.

"I know you are rushed with many demands from all sides, but it doesn't seem right for you not to have at least one house under construction. Especially a house like ours, which could be such a pace setter for the rest of the country. [Note: I believe it was, in fact, the first Wright house to be built after World War II.]

"Are the working drawings completed? When last you spoke of them, about a year ago, I seem to recall you said there was about two days' more work needed to complete them.

"What we'd like especially is to have you stop by and locate the house, barn and road, and tell us how to get started. Katherine promises special hot biscuits for you, if you let us know ahead of time when you're coming."

Not biscuit dough, but the money kind was in Wright's thoughts, because he called me at the office the moment he received my letter, promised to send in his own bulldozer to scoop out the dirt for the sunken garden, and suggested that he would like more money. We had no formal contract with Taliesin, such as we had had for the first house, and in fact we never did have one. I still had received no plans, but I replied as follows, on July 22, 1946:

"Dear Mr. Wright: I'm sorry the telephone connection was so poor this morning that I was not able to understand you well. Besides, I was so flabbergasted by your quick response to my letter that I couldn't collect my wits.

"As I gathered it, you are 'a leetle pressed' right now, and would like additional payment on the plans for the new house.

"I am enclosing a check for $400, which is the best I can do at the moment, because I have not yet completed financing plans for the house to the stage where I can touch the boys for quick money. You will recall that I sent you, I believe in March, 1944, a check for $250, which thus makes a total of $650 on the plans so far. Incidentally, I never did get a floor plan or perspective of the house.

"The bulldozer sounds fine. There's nothing we'd like better than to see the dirt begin to fly."

When he called me at the office, I think Wright suggested the bulldozer as a sort of sweetener, since he was actually asking me to pay for plans that I had never seen, and that were not even finished. His specific request over the telephone was for me to figure out what would be twelve percent of my estimate of the total cost of the house, and send that to him. My earlier payment of two hundred and fifty dollars was undoubtedly spent as soon as received, and he may have forgotten it. Actually, I made no estimate of the total cost, having no bill of materials or other figures to base it on anyway. The four hundred dollars just happened to be the amount I could raise at the moment, and I sent it, hoping that at long last it would produce action. But I was careful in the letter to remind him of the earlier payment.

A prompt thank-you note from him said, "We'll get that floor plan and perspective off to you yet." He promised to stop by, and to send the bulldozer as soon as it was finished at Taliesin. We drove to Taliesin a few days after that note, and Wright told us the bulldozer and driver would be along "in a couple of weeks." With visions of rapid completion dancing in our heads, I scrambled around, still trying to find a city contractor who would take over all the headaches of construction, which seemed to me beyond my capabilities. I found a sympathetic man, but he would take it only on a cost-plus basis. I would have to pay wages from the time the men left his shop until they returned to it. "But they'll work right along when they get on the job?" I asked hopefully. "Oh no," he replied. "They're all just so-so. Nobody seems to want to work hard these days."

I would have become still more downcast, but about that time my brother, a farm real estate agent living ten miles away, turned up a savior in the form of Swiss-born John Luginbuhl, a mason's son who was just out of the army as a paratrooper. He was now running a small farm and doing masonry on the side. He and two other less-skilled farmer masons eventually became our work crew. Then my brother turned up two possible farm quarries, one of them only a mile away. Could they supply the stone we needed?

My excited letter to Wright said, "We're ready for action as fast as you care to push it," and even promised a party for all of

Taliesin if we got into the house by Christmas. This should show that optimism in some people is apparently incurable. I pleaded again for plans, begged him to see whether the quarry stone was suitable, asked for a "bill of materials," so that the quarry owner would know how much stone we wanted.

The bulldozer did not arrive, nor did the plans, and I couldn't even get Wright on the phone. The good building days of summer were melting away fast, and we were getting anxious for action. Finally I resorted to verse, hoping to jolt Wright's sense of humor into action. I give it, to show what desperate weapons a client may feel himself forced to use. Dated August 15, 1946, it reads:

Dear Hard-to-Get-Ahold Of:

> I aint no Rogers Lacy
> And I aint no Johnson (Hib)
> But my life is getting crazy
> And I've trouble with my sib.
>
> Our plans is still in heaven
> We got nothing for to show—
> We are just at six and seven,
> We are feeling mighty low.
>
> There's a guy at Taliesin,
> Daddy Frank, they call his name—
> He is teaching us a lesson
> How to play the patience game.
>
> Who will peek at that old quarry?
> Who will drive a stake in earth?
> Who will stop us being sorry?
> Turn our madness into mirth?
>
> Where's that blueprint of the future?
> Where's the 'dozer with its blade?
> We are waiting with excrutur-
> ating worry. 'Nuff is said.

At least the verse brought prompt results. My Garden Book has this note:

"Fri. Aug. 23, 1946. A big day today. Mr. Wright arrived about 8:45 a.m. after Sue, Elizabeth, Bill and I met him in Middleton. We went over to look at a quarry south of here, and then Mr. Wright staked out the location of the new house, and laid out

the road. John Hill, who drove Mr. Wright over, found two four-leaf clovers. Mr. W. was full of philosophy as well as architecture today. Democracy, said he, is a combination of individuality, creative sensitivity, and individual initiative.

"Dad accidentally located the house. He had gone over earlier, with stakes he had prepared, and drove in a stake on the hilltop to mark where he had laid down his hatchet. Mr. Wright said he thought that was just right for the center of the 'bowl' in front of the house.

"Mr. Wright was especially interested in the way Bill clutched a bouquet of flowers. Maybe their love of beauty is a result of living in that first house, said Mr. W. Or maybe, he added, your own love of beauty led you to have such a house."

Back at the farmhouse, absorbing his seventh biscuit with plenty of homemade butter, he cast a disapproving eye at the ill-planned residence and said, "Katherine, this is awfully practical," meaning that the house was devoid of architectural beauty—or maybe just thinking about the biscuits. Wright took a long look at Bill, who returned his gaze with level eye. Noting a certain similarity, he commented, pointing to Bill and looking at me, "As long as *he* lives, you will never die."

But still no bulldozer. I wrote to Wright on September 16, 1946:

"I'm still blocked in getting a loan because I still don't have the estimates of quantities of materials (particularly lumber) and some idea of costs, which you promised last May to supply. I wrote John Hill over a week ago, asking whether he could supply such figures, but have had no answer . . ."

At last, an entry for October 14, 1946 in my Garden Book declares that we received a building permit that day (the plans had finally been brought in the week before by two Taliesin apprentices), and continues:

"Actual construction of the new house began today with the arrival of the bulldozer from Taliesin, piloted by Joe Stapleton. Bob Elver and Jimmie Grob (two neighbors) did the hauling of the eight-ton machine. Joe gave the boys a demonstration by knocking down two trees and rooting out a stump.

"Tomorrow Joe will start hollowing out the sunken garden, as staked out last week by Wes Peters and John Hill. Johnny Luginbuhl, the mason, is ready to start the wall as soon as we get stone."

15.

Wright Disowns Us

In just three days Joe Stapleton, the bulldozer maestro, carved a new road, scooped out the rough shape of the sunken garden, and cut the floor level of the new house to nearly two feet below grade, pushing the dirt into a ten-foot-high berm at the back. Katherine missed the activities, having taken to her bed in the vain hope of preventing a miscarriage, but by holding up a mirror from her bed was able to get a Lady-of-Shalott-like bird's-eye view. Susan, not quite twelve, stayed out of school to function as cook and nursemaid. Seeing the dirt fly was exciting, for surely we would be in the new house soon after spring rolled round. We did not envision a wait of nearly two years, including, near the halfway point, a potentially disastrous break with Wright that lasted throughout the major portion of the construction.

Who would dig the footings for the crushed rock which Wright had specified instead of the conventional reinforced concrete? Who indeed! Farm boys scorned any labor not involving machines. A contractor with a backhoe said his machine could not straddle the proposed trench because of the berm on one side.

So—on days off and weekends during the fall and the unusually mild early winter I dug down into the red clay by hand (five feet deep and three feet wide when it came to the massive end piers!) and shoveled in and tamped several tons of crushed rock. Now and then the children lent their small hands.

Since the bulldozer was free, thanks to Wright, as were my services, the entire cost of site preparation and footings came to less than twenty dollars, the cost of the crushed rock. In January, 1947, I finished the digging, just before a heavy snow that marooned the farmhouse and part of the neighborhood for four days. In fact for two weeks our farmyard became a transfer point for one neighbor who came with team and bobsled across the fields daily with several cans of milk to meet the milk truck there.

The rest of the winter I chased contractors, unsuccessfully. In the spring I was also finishing my first book—a humorous account of our country living—which contained an incautious sentence that Wright saw later, misinterpreted, and reacted to violently.

Gradually, with so many turndowns, I began to form the idea of becoming my own contractor. I looked with a sharper eye at the working drawings we had. I felt that I could ultimately count on the services of Johnny Luginbuhl, the good mason turned up by my brother, but he still needed plenty of persuasion. We wooed him for months with frequent visits and small presents for his children, until he finally accepted the job—for later. "We'll need a lot of rocks," he said.

In May I took a week off from the newspaper to work in a quarry about six miles away, piling up likely rocks to be trucked to the site; but the owner used dynamite, because he specialized in crushed limestone, so we only got about fifty tons of unshattered rock, far from the four hundred tons that we needed. We had to find another quarry, where the stones were levered out, not dynamited, and we finally turned one up on the farm of a man who raised peas for the local cannery. He eventually delivered all the stone we needed, at three dollars a ton and a dollar for hauling.

That May also marked a busy farming time. Sheep, lambs and cows needed pasture—and the pasture needed fencing, a chronic complaint. Baby chicks were big enough to require a yard built. Elizabeth, just turned eight, gloried in a set of duck eggs under a hen setting in a tub in the kitchen annex. The fuzzy golden down which covered the tiny ducklings when they hatched was a perpetual delight to her. Fortunately her affection for them diminished by the time they were big enough to eat. She raised ducklings for several years after that, as well as becoming a personal friend of every frog, toad and wild animal that she encountered.

The limestone quarry did furnish a small dividend in the form of fossils embedded in some of the stones, which naturally occasioned geological lectures to the children. Mostly the fossils were those of large sea worms, looking like giant screws up to two feet long. We kept them apart when we discovered a more suitable

A bit of child labor helps get crushed rock into the foundation trenches I dug for the walls of the solar house in the winter of 1946-47. The gap in the pile of dirt marks the future location of the tunnel through walls and berm. (Photo by Herbert Jacobs)

quarry, and put them all in the wall of one bedroom. One enormously long stone, when we split it, revealed two prehistoric fish skeletons, each about two feet long. We put it carefully aside, but found too late that one of the masons, no fish lover or fossil admirer, had put it "somewhere" in the wall—he couldn't remember where—after breaking it up.

But this fossil-laying rested in the future, and all we had before us as we drifted into the summer of 1947 were the crushed-rock footings and the huge semi-circle of red clay moved by the bulldozer from the sunken garden and future floor of the house. A rank growth of weeds and grass had already sprung up on it. Two Taliesin apprentices, William Craig and William Wendt, dropped by in the middle of June, and with transit, level and steel tape put in a profusion of small and large stakes to mark the exact dimensions of the stone walls which would be the boundaries of the house. All of the modular unit lines in this house radiated from one central stake in the sunken garden. Happily for me, the

apprentices' measurements coincided almost exactly with my own rough outlines, where I had already put down the foundations of crushed rock. Shaving a few inches off the edges here and there made them conform to the new "official" lines. Such a delightful coincidence made me feel that with enough luck I might succeed after all as a novice contractor.

With the house thus finally staked out, Katherine and I, under Bill Craig's superintending eye, promptly laid up about six square feet of wall, "just to see how it would look." While the creation had that air of splendor which one's own work seems to produce, I was convinced by the sample that my role would be mixing mortar, toting stones and doing other non-skilled tasks, and that I had better leave masonry to the experts.

Besides, other demands were pressing in upon us. I had some pretensions as an amateur water dowser (I did get better at it later, even to the point of taking money), so I "located" the proposed well inside one end of the root cellar we planned to add to the house. A taciturn but efficient well driller began work, but at eighty feet down he hit a slanting flint formation which caused his bit to keep glancing off. And the drill kept getting caught when he tried to pull it up, which meant he was in danger of losing it. He even said that it could not be replaced in those days of post-war scarcity. When Katherine walked over from the farmhouse to see how things were going, the driller and his helper were packing up their rig and getting ready to leave.

Having waited nine months for them to come, she was not going to let that happen without a struggle, so she reminded them of how important it was to us, and asked what they could suggest. The driller replied that if he could choose the location he would start drilling again. He chose a flat area about forty feet south of the house site, saying he could get through any stone in flat layers. Thus he began again, forgiving us any charge for the failure, but now boosting his rate to seven dollars a foot as he went down, and down, and down, some two hundred and forty feet, where he hit a plentiful supply. The new location actually turned out to be more suitable, because the pump would have been noisy in the house, and access to the well shaft difficult for the occasional repairs needed in succeeding years.

When the well driller had finished, he tested the water, under state regulations which then permitted him to claim his whopping

The cement-block barn (which was later stuccoed), with its two big picture windows, was built when the walls of the house were scarcely started, and served for a while as a residence for Katherine's newly-married niece and her husband. They were followed by Jack Steinberg—who took many of the pictures appearing in this book—and his wife Elizabeth. The carport and the trellis beams atop the barn, made from construction planks of the house, were added later. The back of the house is concealed by the barn. (Photo by Herbert Jacobs)

fee. Two of the farmer-masons said they had a rare day to spare "if you have the well pit dug by tomorrow morning." So Katherine and I, in a moonlit evening that lasted until midnight, dug down into that familiar red clay to create a chamber five feet square and seven feet deep, which would hold an electric pump and pressure tank, well below the freezing level. Next day in went cement block walls and a concrete floor, to be followed by a pump and tank, and a concrete cap at ground level.

Not only would we soon have water available for prospective masons, but we had eager users—a just-married niece of Katherine's, who with her husband was already occupying the small barn built just a month before especially for them, turning it into a highly informal bridal suite. Like us, they had found no good place to rent in Madison at a price they could afford. When Katherine suggested that we build the barn immediately and let them live in it, I saw this as an opportunity to draft the bridegroom as a part-time helper on construction of our house. However, aside from helping me roof the barn, there was no other work to do that fall, and they left before the big push began the next spring, for work in another city.

I had trenched a footing for the fourteen-by-twenty-two-foot barn and poured in crushed rock, just as I had done for the big house, but our farmer masons were dubious. They were used to

reinforced concrete for foundations, and thought the cement block walls would surely crack before the barn was even finished. To their surprise (and possibly mine as well) no cracks appeared then or later. I provided a gutter near one end for the future use of cows, and filled it with crushed rock, under a plank which made a temporarily level floor, thus turning the barn into a house rather than a cow palace. Unlike any other barn in the state, it boasted two big plate glass picture windows, each four by five feet, to frame a view of the woods.

When Wright first saw the barn, more than a year later, he was only mildly indignant, and requested that I stucco the outside, and put up planks to form an overhanging trellis for the barn roof. He always insisted in later years that he had never furnished a barn plan, but I claimed that the apprentices had brought in a penciled sketch, which we lost or threw away after the barn was completed. We never did clear up between us a confusion as to whether he really intended a tunnel from house to barn. In the planning stages he suggested frequently that it would be simple to slice a trench about waist deep from house to barn, arch some steel sheets over it, and "just throw some dirt on top." All I could envision of this was a dark, drafty tube, with clammy, crumbling dirt sides, and a leaking roof, the whole making an awkward hump down the middle of the proposed lawn beside the house.

94

The tunnel entrance through the berm was flanked by two flower boxes. Directly above are the small windows of the master bedroom; the upper part of the circular tower at the right houses the bathroom. The small pipes sticking up out of the berm lead to oil tanks buried in it. Trees and shrubs covered the berm in later years. (Photo © Ezra Stoller)

But in his set of plans Wright had designed an above-ground tunnel of stone through the berm at the back of the house, graced at its outside end by two large stone flower boxes. That was the plan we followed.

Perhaps we did not press for clarification on the tunnel because we wanted to add to the house an underground room that was not in Wright's plan. It would be a solution to the problem left hanging when Wright did nothing about Katherine's request for a separate rear entrance to the house, which was intended to keep farm dirt and clothes away from the front door. As we studied the plans we noticed that the back wall of the kitchen, the bulge of the utility room, and the side wall of the tunnel through the berm made three sides of a room. All it would need would be a fourth wall, a concrete roof, and a floor; and it would be completely covered by the dirt berm. I put in a shallow footing, and when our farmer-mason friends ran up the walls of the barn I had them put in a six-foot cement block wall for our root cellar and storage room. Later I had the masons leave a door opening at the middle of the stone tunnel through the berm.

The door off the tunnel gave an entrance through the earth or root cellar (we used both names) to the circular utility room off the kitchen. I hung my barn jacket and overalls there, and shed my dirty boots. Here we stored and washed dirty clothes, as well as the milk utensils. "It was a room I was thankful for but never proud of," Katherine comments.

As soon as it was laid up, the wall served as a mount for the well pump switch, and for a box to contain the fuses and circuit breakers of the future house wiring system. Wright did not want electric wires spoiling the silhouette of the house, so the cables came underground, via the side of the barn, from a transformer on a post behind the barn. Thus were aesthetics taken care of.

Our hopes leapt skyward on August 14, 1947 when the elusive mason, Johnny Luginbuhl, arrived with two helpers, and the stones began to fly. By good luck it was my day off from the paper, and Katherine and I spent it rushing bags of cement and lime from the old farm barn to the little gasoline-powered mixer (for mixing mortar) which Johnny had wheeled up behind his car. Since the well was still not provided with a pump, we rushed water in milk cans, and in between times toted stones to the busy masons. We could, just could, get into that house by Christmas,

we figured. I noted in a Garden Book entry that the men "laid more stone in one day than we thought possible." In two days they had outlined the whole house with a ribbon just one stone high—nestled on a bed of mortar on the rock fill—and had also built up more of the corner that Katherine and I had started nearly two months earlier.

And then they vanished. Visits to Johnnie's farm proved unproductive. He wore his usual engaging smile, but would say only, "I'll be back when I get more time." It could have been the sudden request of a neighbor that he build a new milkhouse or repair a barn foundation, or maybe just a piling up of farm work. We did learn that he had gone to Taliesin to look at the stonework there, and had concluded, "I can do that."

Toward the end of October Johnny did come back, but only for a day. He ran up more of the tunnel wall, and I was the helper, mixing mortar and hauling stones. Toward midafternoon a light rain began, the mortar would no longer "set up," and we had to quit. "First thing next spring," Johnnie said brightly, and we had to be content with that. Aware that nobody would want to lay up stone on that wintry hilltop during the winter, we decided there was nothing else we could do. Besides, at that time I was highly involved in revising the manuscript of my first book along the lines of the publisher's suggestions, and to a beginning author probably no earthly cataclysm outranks his book in importance.

Wright was sympathetic over our delay, and even mildly enthusiastic about my book project. He offered to furnish a drawing of the new house as a frontispiece for the book, and even sent it immediately, before he and the Taliesinites made their annual fall trek to the Arizona Taliesin. I was kept busy with the interminable series of letters to and from the publisher, and with all the other correspondence which that kind of venture seems to provoke. I had also started a weekly column for the paper, writing it at home for extra pay. In early February I happily corrected three successive batches of proofs for the book, bursting with pride as I did so, and making a special point of returning them by the next day's mail.

Unknown to me, the publisher had also sent a set of proofs to Wright, doubtless hoping for some sparkling comment that could be used on the dust jacket or in publicity releases. But Wright's eye fell on what I had considered a wholly innocent sentence near the end of the book, put in merely to explain why he had gone to the trouble of driving in from Taliesin one Sunday to pick us up. The sentence read: "Even before moving to the farm we had set things in motion by causing Wright to drive us past the new location, on a day when he sought my help in going over the manuscript of the new version of his autobiography." I had not even thought it worthwhile to add that in less than an hour of looking at a few pages, I had found that I could make no acceptable suggestions, and the matter had been dropped.

Wright interpreted the phrase "going over the manuscript" to mean that I was saying that he sought my help in writing it. He withdrew permission to the publisher to use the drawing of the house, and from bitter comments on the galley proofs, which he returned to me instead of to the publisher, and in a letter which followed the proofs, I realized that I would be on my own as far as Wright — and Taliesin — were concerned in getting that house built. I studied the plans with renewed attention, for we were determined to carry them out faithfully.

16.

The Spring Surge

Such was our confidence in Johnny Luginbuhl's smiling promise that he would "be back next spring to finish this up," that we sold the old barn and farmhouse, plus three acres surrounding it, in February, 1948, while everything was still under heavy snow. We even promised to be out of the place by July 1. Still believing in miracles, we thought the new house might be sufficiently finished by that time so that we could move into at least a part of it. And if that proved impossible, we were going to pitch a tent near the building site, and manage somehow.

We hadn't waited for the first Wright house to be finished before moving in, and saw no reason to change our pattern. Besides, as my own contractor it was beginning to dawn on me that I would need working capital to pay for materials as well as workmen. Improvident as I was, I had no firm commitment from any lending company to pick up the inevitable mortgage when it would become necessary. I thought of the Haley brothers and their building and loan company, and how nobly they had stepped in to finance the first house, thanks to Harry Haley's warm memories of Wright's Chicago Midway Gardens. Though they were a bit dubious of anything "out in the country," they took only a day to approve a fifteen-thousand-dollar loan, to be available when needed. Of course by this time we had given up any idea that this large house could be built for anything near five thousand dollars.

I had paid for the well, the new barn, and some other materials from my newspaper salary, which had been possible because the farm became debt-free when I sold off some surplus acreage early in the game. I had already been squirreling away needed supplies, still difficult to obtain in the immediate post-war years. Not realizing that it would cake with age (though a few whacks with a sledge broke it up easily), I kept acquiring small quantities of ce-

ment, until I found I had a total of eighty bags. Another bargain, which I picked up at a lumber yard, consisted of about thirty rough planks, each sixteen feet long, which served at various times as scaffolding, braces, concrete forms, tracks on which to slide heavy objects, wheelbarrow paths, benches, and temporary shelves. The planks that survived ended as an overhanging trellis at both ends of the barn. Bristling with slivers, they were unfinished, a full two inches thick (instead of the customary inch-and-a-half thickness of "two-inch" planks), and so heavy that a single plank was all one man could carry.

When Wright furnished a layout for the floor heating pipes I sent it off to the Chicago firm he recommended, and in a few months got some hundreds of feet of two-inch wrought iron pipe, already curved to fit the curve of the house. Each piece was clearly numbered with yellow paint to show where it would go in the detailed layout. The planks, cement and pipes were all stored in the driveway of the old barn on the farm, sharing the interior with cows, steers, sheep, and a few dozen chickens. During the spring a couple of baby pigs played in the straw around the pipes, coming out at milking time to be fed. They managed to get a lot of straw into the pipes, but it all seemed to shake out before the pipes were welded together.

The great day came the last week in March, when Johnny the mason arrived, a blond, lithe, under-thirty, alert craftsman, still with the springy tread of his paratrooper days, a precisionist in every movement. His helper was a hulking six-footer named Barthel Zurbuchen, who was Swiss like Johnny, but slower and mostly unsmiling.

Uncovered at last from the snow, the tracery of stones which outlined the house looked like those pitiful foundations unearthed by archeologists, from which one is supposed to imagine great pillared temples with spacious porticoes. Under Johnny's masterful and creative approach as the stone walls began rapidly rising, the scene swiftly changed to resemble a picture of war's destruction. On the clay floor lay the debris of rock fragments, planks leading to the heaps of stones near the portions of wall—which looked as if they had been bombed down, rather than being in the process of going up. In the background, withered weeds, soon interspersed with green shoots, covered the curve of the berm behind "the works."

We soon fell into a pattern. I had already hauled to the site a

The walls of the circular tower are nearing their sixteen-foot height, and show the outer and inner layers of stone. Insulating material was poured between the two layers. The three farmer masons are Albert Hinze, a neighbor, at left; Bartel Zurbuchen, foreground, putting a nailing plate into the wall; and beyond him Johnny Luginbuhl, the master mason. The completed fourteen-foot height of the east pier and adjoining tower appear behind Johnny, ready for roofing. In the distance, my father surveys the garden with the children, and I can be seen at the mortar mixer near the tool shack. (Photo by Jack Steinberg)

tarpaper shelter that I had built for chickens a few years earlier, to serve as storehouse for bags of cement, lime and tools. Each morning, after milking the cows and doing other farm chores, I would toss a few bags of cement into the trunk of the car and drop them off at the site, on my way to work. If I happened to be smart that morning I would slip on a pair of overalls for the loading and unloading. If not, I relied on patting and the wind to remove the cement dust before I got to the office.

A few minutes later, at about 7:30, Johnny and a succession of helpers would arrive. Johnny always wore a white-visored cap and started each day with a fresh pair of white canvas gloves. Each night, when he quit at six o'clock, he would toss the dirty, ragged pair of gloves into the trash can with a ceremonial gesture. And every night the masons tossed their trowels and long-tailed hammers into a bucket of water, so that the handles would swell during the night and fit tight. The books say to keep the handles dry and well wedged, because soaking soon crushes the wood fibers, but these masons had always soaked their hammers, and they were not about to change.

Katherine watched for the arrival of the workmen in the morning and went over to the site to make sure that the cement mixer worked, that all workmen were present, and that nobody had any questions. Then she returned for some quick housework, because she had a job waiting for her at the site, which she had carved out for herself. Toward mid-morning, with the children off to school, she would walk over to the construction site from the farmhouse and start raking joints. She had noticed the masons using the tips of their trowels to rake or gouge out the mortar as much as half an inch, so that the stones would stand out, and the mortar be unobtrusive. We knew that Wright wanted to achieve the effect of a stylized quarry wall by having the mortar raked out and the stones laid with some of them sticking out a bit and some recessed, rather than having a smooth face. He had done the same thing in the first house, emphasizing the horizontal lines of the bricks and wooden walls. In the second house, the mortar dried to virtually the same color as the limestone, so there was no need for a separate vertical mortar color.

Katherine found that small, slightly pointed sticks of wood worked better for her than the heavy mason's trowels. Not only did she take over a task that the masons disliked, but her working

Master mason Johnny Luginbuhl surveys placement of a thin stone "newspaper" near the top of the wall. The wall pattern accommodated stones of all sizes and shapes, with little trimming. (Photo by Jack Steinberg)

alongside them and often encouraging them with praise had the added effect of speeding up the stone laying. In fact, these honest toilers seemed to have the goal of seeing just how much stone they could lay in a day. She also expounded Wright's ideas about architecture and this house in particular, and thus gave them a sense of participation, while she superintended unobtrusively.

Johnny Luginbuhl was the only expert mason, the others being semi-skilled. He asked two dollars an hour, and the others a dollar eighty, and they worked six days a week, without overtime. Toward the end Johnny raised his pay to two dollars and a quarter, and the others to two dollars, but in view of their good performance (and the fact that they were nearly finished) I did not protest. None of them wanted to work in the city, partly because they distrusted unions.

Johnny had said, "We'll run up those walls in three weeks," but it was actually three months before they finished. The crew vanished for a few days in early April to plant oats, and again in late May to seed corn. In June they took another break, for the first cutting of hay. The work went fairly fast because the masons had to do very little trimming of the stone. Now and then they would lop the end off a stone with one expert blow of the hammer to square it up, or would flatten a bulging top, but they did none of the elaborate stone-trimming which runs up the labor cost.

Since it was freshly quarried and arrived on a flatbed dump truck two or three times a week, the stone was still soft to work, hardening later on contact with the air. The huge walls cost about fifteen hundred dollars for stone, and an equal amount to lay the stone up. The walls, plus the glass and wood roof, represented almost the total cost of the shell of the house. As with the first house, it was a single operation, requiring no further expense.

We had acquired by that time a second car, used and indeed ancient. And if our masons needed more lime, gasoline for the mortar mixture, or any other supplies, Katherine was on hand to run errands. Anything to keep them steadily at work.

About 4:30 each afternoon Katherine would appear with a pan of frosted cake and a bottle of beer for everybody. And that was money well spent! Elizabeth, then just nine years old, fondly remembers the beer and cake breaks. She and William, not yet five, would tag along to the building site, where the masons, as the treat appeared, would put down their tools and chat and laugh for a few minutes. Occasionally she would be allowed to bake the cake herself, and present it proudly to the appreciative work crew. It was their only break all day, aside from half an hour at noon to eat the lunches they brought from home. After the cake and beer they attacked the stones with more zeal than before, working steadily until six, when they went home for milking and other chores. Katherine had about an hour's work after they left, raking the last of the joints laid, before returning to the farmhouse to make supper.

Beginning in February I had taken on an extra job, teaching a news writing class twice a week at the university on my way home. Other days I usually got home about five, and then spent time piling up more stones at the spot where the men were working, or boosting stones up onto scaffolds. In the evening Katherine and I checked the plans to make sure she could tell Johnny the next morning about leaving holes for beam ends, nailing plates for partitions, embedding bolts in the masonry for flitchplates or window frames, and other construction variations. I was helped in my stone moving by a big pneumatic rubber wheel for the wheelbarrow. These wheels were just coming into use, along with ball-bearing axles, and Katherine thought the twelve dollars and a half was an extravagance, but my back highly approved of it.

The back wall and the circular utility room/bathroom wall were both eighteen inches thick, which worked out usually to a stone at the front side and one on the back side, with a three- to four-inch space between them. The massive end walls or piers were three feet thick, narrowing to eighteen inches at their centers. On these end walls, both of them with outside exposures to the weather, the masons filled the hollow space with vermiculite as insulation, bridging across with metal ties and an occasional stone to bind the two sides of the wall together. They built the back wall solid, tossing in broken pieces of stone, and misshapen stones which they called "crips" (for cripples) to fill the space. Since the back wall would have the berm pushed up against it for all but the last two feet, they only insulated the exposed portion.

Johnny usually did the wall faces that would show, while the assistants laid the stones that would be covered or seldom seen. Although they worked steadily, the men did a lot of joshing and bantering. Their favorite joke, which seemed to keep them in constant good humor, was "laying newspapers." These were very thin stones, laid sometimes two and even three tiers high, to level up a section, or occasionally to give some variety to the face. The men had rapidly grasped the concept of a "stylized quarry wall," and would compare one wall section with another, to make sure they were maintaining a uniform style. The "newspaper stones," however, remained their favorite gag, and they liked to point them out to me when I got back late in the day from my newspaper job. In addition to the fossil stones in another room, in our own bedroom I embedded a terra cotta plaque given to me by an American abstract sculptor with whom I had traveled in Spain and Italy nearly twenty years earlier.

We weren't the only ones laying up treasures. When the masonry was nearly finished, a small white streak under the roof, and nearly thirteen feet up in the air, puzzled me. Johnny Luginbuhl explained with a shy smile, "That's my trademark, a small piece of white marble that I put in every building, somewhere, when I'm near to finishing." I smiled myself, remembering that Wright had embedded bits of broken Japanese statuary and pottery in the rebuilt walls of Taliesin after the two ruinous fires.

While the walls were going up I sought to anticipate next steps. I found a steamfitter who would be ready to weld the heating pipes and put in a furnace as soon as the floor area was cleared of the debris of stones and a bed of crushed rock had been laid

Katherine cleans out mortar from the stones of what will be the stairwell to the mezzanine floor. The holes above her head are for the ends of roof rafters. Albert Hinze, a mason, is standing on the concrete roof of the earth cellar. (Photo by Jack Steinberg)

down. The plumber who had helped put a flush toilet in the farmhouse after the end of the war was saving bathroom fixtures for me. But our best find was a small-time cabinetmaker and building contractor named Wilfred Way, who, with a son and one skilled helper, agreed to do the huge door-window frames and all the glasswork under contract, as well as build the roof and the mezzanine floor. With Wright and all the Taliesin apprentices out of the picture I had been afraid I would be out of my depth if I had to try to interpret the drawings on the millwork for the windows, the intricate layout of beams and joists for the mezzanine, and the giant roof overhangs at both ends of the house. Way looked at the plans and smiled. "They are very easy to follow. I'm sure I won't have any trouble."

As the walls moved slowly upward, and it became rather certain that we would never be able to meet the July 1 deadline to give up the farmhouse and still have a new roof to shelter under, the pro-

spective root cellar began to look like a good alternative. I directed the masons to finish the walls of the tunnel through the berm, and the kitchen and utility room walls up to at least seven feet. Sam Parisi, an intense, painstaking and imaginative young cement contractor from the nearby village of Middleton, quickly floored the root cellar, sprouted a forest of support posts on it, and poured a roof that also covered the tunnel. I had provided a series of heavy bolts in the masonry, to anchor the roof to the kitchen wall.

I had already hauled a foot-wide iron pipe out from Madison and helped to set it up as the furnace flue, and it towered some sixteen feet in the air—well above the incomplete masonry—held against wind and storm by guy wires. Wright had planned for it to be only half concealed inside the wall, the exposed portion being intended to heat the second floor bathroom. Although it did furnish some heat, it would not have been enough for that large room, and I had arranged with the steamfitter to put in a radiator.

The masons had virtually completed all the stonework when this picture was taken at the end of June, 1948. The fireplace opening is in the center, and the boarded opening from the stairs to the mezzanine is above it and to the right. Holes for both mezzanine beams and roof supports show in the circular bathroom/utility room tower. The lower part of the wall to right of the tower is mortared smooth for the backs of the kitchen cupboards. (Photo by Herbert Jacobs)

Katherine found the building of the huge fireplace chimney the most challenging part of the stonework, perhaps because she was right there all the time to check the measurements and progress, and to reassure Johnny. The fireplace opening, six feet wide and five feet high, provided no special problems, but the chimney flue, lined with massive tiles a foot-and-a-half in diameter, had to slant three feet almost immediately to meet and become part of the circular bathroom/utility room stone wall, close to the furnace pipe. And inside the slanting flue Johnny had to make room for a big circular damper disc. The slant to the bathroom/utility room wall was necessary to avoid obscuring the first window of the band of windows that circled the bedroom wall just under the roof.

A flat steel plate, instead of the traditional masonry arch, carried the weight of the stones above the fireplace opening, but perhaps from force of habit Johnny cut and inserted a keystone in the first row of stones. Extending up into the next layer, it marred the symmetry of the horizontal lines, but he was so proud of it

that we said nothing. We had gone over the measurements on the plans several times, and checked them with Johnny, but he let it be known that no one was to speak to him or even watch while he was wrestling with the slant of the chimney.

He worked in total silence and concentration all that day, but when the workmen left Katherine worried that the opening looked much too large. Indeed, prisoners tunneling under a jail wall would have found it ample, when Johnny finished. She checked the measurements, but found Johnny had carried them out exactly. The next day, as utility wall and chimney rose together, it all began to look quite right, as we discovered again and again in carrying out the plans. A thin skin of stones covered the outside of the tiles. The fireplace and furnace flues both ended flush with the top of the bathroom wall, which was itself nearly three feet above the main roof, so no chimney was visible, and the result was the massive masonry effect that Wright sought so often.

During the construction period, and before we had moved in,

This "beering-out party" marked the last day of masonry and the completion of the walls near the end of June, 1948. Johnny Luginbuhl, chief mason, is in the right foreground, with his white cap pushed onto the back of his head, and Katherine is between Bartel Zurbuchen and Albert Hinze, mason and close neighbor, with three young helpers. Besides scraping out the fresh mortar joints, Katherine furnished a beer and cake break for the workmen every afternoon. (Photo by Jack Steinberg)

we liked to drive over at night, park in the field near the edge of the sunken garden, and gaze at those massive walls, so like a dream castle, in the glare of the headlights. As one walked around inside it, the place resembled a great theater stage. Several times, eager and interested visitors joined us on these nocturnal jaunts.

I had the masons run up the rest of the walls of the bathroom, and Wilfred Way then rapidly put in a bathroom floor, stairs, and a roof. Since the bathroom had no windows, Wright had designed an elaborate skylight for its center, but Way and I decided to build something much simpler. For a month, however, the opening was merely covered with a tarpaulin while Way went ahead with other construction.

The July 1 deadline for moving came and went, and the new farmhouse owner, a very obliging ex-GI with a wife and one small child, gave us another week's grace. During that interval the plumber put in the bathroom fixtures, and added a toilet under the stairs and a sink in the utility room. He put in a hot water heater, connected the house pipes to the pump, and laid soil pipes to a septic tank which we had already excavated and built near the barn. Sam Parisi, the cement wizard, had put a floor in the utility room, leaving a channel where the heating pipes would be installed later.

Just as we were about to move into the root cellar of the half-finished house, a member of the Chicago Symphony orchestra who had been spending musical summers at Taliesin, and whom we had met casually, phoned me that Wright had now apparently "forgiven" us. We were to come out the next Sunday morning for a friendly meeting that he said he had arranged with Wright.

But either our friend grossly misunderstood, or Wright had suddenly changed his views. When we drove to Taliesin and were admitted to the old drafting room, Wright once more expressed his bitter feeling about my book, and refused to accept my apologetic explanations. But now he also accused us of "destroying" his concept of the building by failing to carry out the plans properly. We asked why he thought that was the case, and he replied that "the boys" had reported this to him. We could not accept such an opinion after working so hard and faithfully in carrying out the plans.

Katherine finally said, "Mr. Wright, this is the first time we have known you to take someone else's word for something. We wish you would come in and see for yourself. We have followed the plans very faithfully." On that we left, hurt and unhappy because we had hoped that when he returned to Wisconsin from the winter in Arizona Wright would find that we were building the house as he had planned, and would enjoy its excitement with us.

When electric lights, hot and cold running water, and even a telephone were installed and functioning, we moved into the root cellar and the silo (as we called the utility room/bathroom stack) on Thursday, July 8, my day off. Bob Elver, the trucker who lived down the road a bit, brought our upright piano on a flatbed truck, and played a tune as he arrived. It probably should have been "Hail! Hail! The Gang's All Here!" but his repertoire was limited.

In early June Katherine and the masons were high on a scaffold, completing the stonework of the circular tower, with a field of oats just pushing through the soil in the foreground. (Photo by Jack Steinberg)

We were as snugly packed as the crew of a submarine. What we managed to stuff into the small cellar included the piano, a large refrigerator, a four-foot-wide deep-freeze locker, an oil stove, two sets of bookcases which served as shelves, and beds for two of the children. We still had room to set up two card tables for meals, with the beds serving as seats. A third child had a cot in the utility room. Katherine's eighteen-year-old nephew, Bruce Hotchkiss, there to help us for the summer, slept in a tent at the edge of the woods.

Katherine and I had our beds in the bathroom on the second floor of the utility room. With its sixteen-foot diameter, and unencumbered as yet by partitions or closets, the room had plenty of space for all the fixtures plus the two beds. We used electric light to see by, because the tarpaulin covered the future skylight

opening, and the two doorways in the walls were boarded up until the mezzanine floor construction began. When a storm struck one night, being in that open-air structure was like being in the prow of a ship.

First things first! Either the first or second night in our new home, I don't remember which, we mixed a bucket of mortar and cemented a stone hearth for the fireplace, extending it out in the fan shape set forth in the plans. We had already selected and placed the stones, so the mortaring took only about an hour. The next night, not waiting for any longer curing process, we had our first fireplace fire, and the whole family sat around on sawhorses and nail kegs to enjoy it. The flames cast a surprisingly ruddy glow over the limestone walls, with fascinating pockets of light and shadow because of the uneven surfaces. Above us shone a

Heating pipes rest in their bed of crushed rock and forms are in place for the inside pool and living room floor just before the pouring of concrete in early July, 1948. Beyond the west pier with its full-length slot window the beginnings of the terrace which circled the front of the house have been laid. The hole for the outside half-circular plunge pool was dug soon after the floor was poured. (Photo by Jack Steinberg)

Long two-by-six rafters, to provide for both front and back roof overhangs, are in place here atop the fourteen-foot mullions. Laid out with transit and steel tape, from a post in the center of the sunken garden, each rafter represented the segment of an arc. The portion of terrace laid near the front door appears at lower right. (Photo by Jack Steinberg)

Some of the first of two layers of roof boards are already in place, and rafters have been strengthened with one-by-twelve boards spiked to their sides. Steel rods hang from the rafters, ready to support the outer ends of floor beams for the mezzanine. (Photo by Jack Steinberg)

brilliant canopy of stars, undimmed by street lights. Obviously, we felt, Wright knew what he was doing when he made the fireplace the central element of his houses. We had a fire every night from then on.

During the time of settling in, of course, we found plenty to do. While the steamfitter was welding and leveling the floor heating pipes, I dug the clay out for the inside pool, and put in forms for it and for the wall separating it from the outside plunge pool. I measured, and put forms in place—properly braced—for pouring the concrete floor, and built a timber causeway for the readymix truck to get close enough to spout concrete into small carts for distribution.

On a steaming Saturday in mid-July Sam Parisi and his crew poured most of the floor, but before Parisi would lay the top inch he got into a row with the mixer driver over the quality of the mix. Pouring forth a string of rich Italian oaths, he refused any further

concrete, and insisted that the truck return Sunday morning with a mix that he specified. With feelings eventually smoothed over, this was done.

To determine the square footage of the floor, in the absence of any help from Taliesin, I had gone a fast and rugged round with my high school mathematics, calculating areas of large and small circles, and subtracting, to get the area of the house floor for a segment of an arc seventeen feet wide. I checked it by laying off rectangles from the drawing and then piecing together the long triangles from between them. When I was satisfied that I was approximately correct, I offered the figure to Parisi, but he had his pride to consider. "I'll figure this out myself," he said loftily. The next day he came around, with a sheepish smile, and said, "Say, what was that figure you told me yesterday? That's close enough for my purposes." It worked out to be about three hundred dollars, which I considered reasonable. Just before the cement

The roof is completed, the mezzanine floor and walkway parapet are in place, and the carpenters are setting up a moveable scaffold which they will use in installing the framed plate glass of the upper tier of fixed windows. (Photo by Jack Steinberg)

finally hardened, Parisi's men gave the floor what is called a "hard finish," troweling with great sweeping motions, using the edges of their steel trowels while they crawled around on kneepads. We had hoped to put red color into the top layer, but Parisi could not get a satisfactory mix with the color, and that idea had to be abandoned. Later we applied colored wax, but the floor finish was so hard that most of the wax rubbed off in areas of heavy use and had to be reapplied.

Scarcely had the floor been laid than Wilfred Way began transforming our medieval stone castle into a house. Soon two- by six-inch mullions rose fourteen feet, at six-foot intervals, to meet the rafters, which were themselves a special fabricated beam of Wright's design, an ingenious economy. He specified two- by six-inch lumber for the rafters, which had to be twenty-four feet long to provide for a roof overhang at front and back. Inside the house, between the mullions and the back wall, each rafter had

a one- by twelve-inch board nailed to each side, which gave, in addition to outward thrust, a very strong bearing, both for the roof and for the steel rods which hung from the rafters to hold up the outer ends of the mezzanine beams. Visitors later were amazed at Wright's bold use of wood. The overhangs at each end, with their flitch plates, had an intricate rafter pattern.

Within a week Way and his two helpers had finished the roof—and solved another cost problem. Wright's plans called for a pitch and gravel roof with a wide piece of copper flashing at its front edge, but Way found that such a copper strip would cost over a thousand dollars. Why not just fold the top edge of the tar-paper behind a fascia board, he suggested. Cheap and effective, and Way achieved the bending of the fascia board into the sharp curve of the roof by a series of vertical sawcuts on its inside edge to permit the bending. Completion was almost in sight—but a new storm was about to break.

17.

From Cellar to Solar

When the mezzanine was completed, we moved out of the earth cellar and began using the whole house, though it was occasionally a bit breezy without glass. Kitchen cabinets and counter, with stove and icebox in place, made cooking easier. (Photo by Jack Steinberg)

Before we could congratulate ourselves on all this progress, a new and deadly peril appeared in the shape of the finance firm's loan committee, which came with teeth bared and ears laid back. Apparently they had just discovered that I had no general overall contract price to shelter under, in this new-fangled oddity of a building designed by a locally distrusted architect. I tagged along beside them, trying to sell the idea that the house was actually very close to completion, which was true. With the roof on, and the mezzanine well along, the only other major item would be the doors and other windows, plus a couple of hundred dollars for boards for the partitions I would build during the winter.

They couldn't and wouldn't believe it. Steeped in the ancient ways, they pictured expensive cabinets, closets and window trim, false and hardwood floors, wiring, heating and plumbing, all usually added at this point, but not visible here.

"Understand you're even planning a swimming pool," one of the loan committee had jibed. "Is this it?" he said, pointing scornfully to the sunken garden, which was awash in stray boards and empty cement bags. "Well, it's really just a small plunge pool," I tried to explain, but he pushed on, unheeding. The verdict came the next morning by telephone: "We're going to sell you out right away, and try to salvage what we can."

I took my troubles to my brother, a farm real estate agent who had arranged details of the loan. With a reassuring smile he said, "They'll back down. Some of that collateral which they accepted would not meet state requirements, and I will take pleasure in reminding them of that fact." He did, and they backed, and we had no more trouble. In fact, a year later, when I had finished the interior work, we had the whole finance company office and sales force out for an office party.

Although I had not pointed it out to the loan committee man, we had already begun digging for the outside pool, which was to be a twelve-foot half-circle against the wall of the inside pool. In three or four days it was completed. Katherine laid up the curve of the wall with old "crip" stones rejected by the masons. I put in a simple drain to the sand of the sunken garden. We paid a mason ten dollars to plaster the inside of the curve with waterproof cement, and floor it, and the pool was done! It was promptly put to use, to the huge delight of the children. And after milking the cows and tending to the other animals I would strip and have a plunge myself, both morning and evening. To be sure, two strokes get you from one end to the other, but it furnished a refreshing dip twice a day. If friends dared to speak derisively of its dimensions, I would counter with "And how big is *your* pool?"

We had moved the animals with us from the farm, fencing in

109

By early August of 1948 the plunge pool was filled and in daily use by the children. The separate inside pool, only eighteen inches deep, was not filled and planted until late fall. (Photo by Herbert Jacobs)

part of the hillside back of the house for the sheep, and continuing the cow and beef animals in the fields around the house, with an electric fence so unobtrusive that the animals looked as if they were roaming free just beyond the sunken garden. By the time cold weather came the young couple who had moved into the barn when Katherine's niece left were also gone, and the barn at last became a place for animals instead of humans.

After the house roof was installed, we brought over the gas stove, which ran on bottled gas and had replaced the old coal and wood stove in the farmhouse. We could now do without the oil stove in the root cellar, but we still ate breakfast and lunch there, since flies, because of the nearness of animals, were such a pest. By evening the flies subsided, and we ate at a table eight feet long

which I had copied by memory from the dining table in our first Wright house. Not until ten years later did I get around to building the eight-foot hexagonal version that Wright had designed for this second house, together with the elaborate sideboard and shelves against which the table fitted.

Like the roof joists, the beams to support the mezzanine floor were fashioned on the job. Each consisted of parallel two-by-sixes, spiked to a two-by-four laid flat between them. Alternate beams, into which the support rods from the roof fitted, carried two two-by-fours. I had allowed generous holes in the wall for the beams, so Katherine had plenty to do, filling and mortaring around them with small stones once they were in place. Wright's original plans had called for double flooring, but his second set eliminated elaborate framing, and provided a much simpler two-inch planking with splines—thin strips of wood fitted into slots in the sides of the planks. Way's power saw cut the slots, with considerable saving over tongue-and-groove planks.

A delightful dividend came in the shape of five hexagonal tables of Wright's design, put together by Way for ten dollars each from the salvaged ends of the planks. Four were eighteen inches high; and one, the height of a dining table, we used for a breakfast table in the kitchen, and as an occasional extension of the dining table. Katherine finished them with a very durable clear sealer to keep the natural wood color and make them stain-proof. She used the same material on all the woodwork, inside and out.

Wright, chilly but civil, came back into the picture briefly by telephone on a Saturday morning in mid-August. I was scheduled to work as city editor of the paper that night, but carpenter Way found himself stumped, and appealed to me. He was about to fit a short beam into the bulge of the utility room wall to support the mezzanine floor at its narrowest point. "But the plans don't show any rod to the roof to support the outside end," he complained. I decided to call Wright for guidance.

Wright explained briskly. "That beam is to be cantilevered," he said. "Drive the hole all the way through the wall, slantwise, put in the beam, and cover the end with a thin layer of stone on the inside of the wall." Simple. And why didn't we think of it? I had time, before going to the office, to chisel out the hole, and realized as I did so that with a hole going slantwise into an eighteen-inch wall there was plenty of bearing to cantilever the beam for

The full sweep of the living room, dining area and kitchen appears here. Although the space was completely open, the curve of the house seemed to create "phantom partitions" and to divide the space into rooms. The hexagonal tables of Wright's design, made from the ends of mezzanine planks, were ordinarily placed at the edge of the inside pool as suggested by Wright, but were moved by the photographer for this picture. (Photo © Ezra Stoller)

Posed by a newspaper photographer, the family appears here some time after the living room was completed. Susan is in the distance at the piano, while Elizabeth and William are on the floor near the inside pool. Katherine and I made the easy chair—one of a pair—from memory, patterning it after the chairs in our first Wright house. (Photo by James Roy Miller)

adequate support, since the balcony was only four feet wide at that point, which was just outside the master bedroom.

When the mezzanine-balcony and the three-foot-high parapet at its front were finished by the end of August, we moved the beds there while Way began carefully installing the glass doors and windows which would close up the house. A simple curtain partitioned off the master bedroom, but the children lived in dormitory style, their three small empires of beds and possessions scattered the sixty-foot length of the mezzanine. One violent rainstorm discomfited them for a night, when the wind blew minor torrents through the gap left for windows above the back wall, and we moved their beds to the shelter of the bathroom wall. I took most of the winter to finish partitioning the bedrooms.

Life was easier in our expanded but still airy quarters under the big roof, but we still found plenty to do. Katherine and I completed the stone terrace that she and her nephew had been laying, which extended six feet along the front of the house and spread out under the corner overhangs. Instead of a concrete foundation we simply laid down a bed of sand and fitted the four-inch-thick stones loosely together, pouring grout in the cracks between them. I was certain that just walking on them would tilt the stones and crack the mortar, and the first winter's frost would doubtless heave a few. But luck was apparently with us, and the terrace stones remained intact year after year, with none needing repair or replacement.

Wilfred Way was taking his time on the windows, but since it was a contract price, I remained quite calm. As in the first house it was all culled plate—old store windows cut up—but I noticed no

The mezzanine balcony looked something like a disorganized dormitory until partitions were installed. Each child set up a bed and grouped possessions in the area where his future bedroom was to be. (Photo by Jack Steinberg)

A sunny noon in mid-November shows how the sun came far into the house at that season. This is the view of house and sunken garden which guests and visitors had when they came through the tunnel and walked around the corner. The slope of the sunken garden began at the edge of the six-foot terrace. Capped by transoms, the east and west end doors were six and a half feet high, at our request to Wright—small enough to be handled easily by children the size of Elizabeth and William, who are seated here beside the pool. The wide overhang at the west end was supported by flitch plates (steel plates bolted to wood) fastened to bolts anchored deep in the masonry. (Photo © Ezra Stoller)

Still bare of planting when this picture was taken, the berm rose up against the back of the house almost to the row of bedroom windows under the roof. The sunken garden at the front, the semi-circular shape of the house, and the slope of the berm combined to produce an airfoil which cut the force of the cold southwest winds of winter. The berm also protected the living room and part of the bedroom walls, keeping them cool in summer and warm in winter. The back of the house faced north and overlooked pasture and woods which sloped to the highway. (Photo © Ezra Stoller)

gold leaf anywhere. The upper panels, above the nine-foot break, were all in fixed frames. The pairs of doors below alternated with fixed panels. The end doors were only six and a half feet high, with ventilation transoms above, because we had asked Wright for something smaller there, that a child could handle. Way had the whole house enclosed by the end of September, just ahead of the nippy fall weather.

A few days after Way had finished all the windows, we looked out as we were about to sit down to Sunday lunch, and there was Wright, standing at the edge of the sunken garden, looking at the house! Not knowing his mood, I opened the door and said, "Why don't you come in and look around?"

Not a word was said then or later about his eight months of hostility as he walked in. He toured the house, offering some suggestions but no real criticism, and appearing relieved. He ignored the fact that all had been done without Taliesin supervision. I explained that I would be working during the rest of the fall and winter, putting in the partitions for the bedrooms, and building the cabinets and other built-in furniture specified in the plans. Katherine did have a fresh apple pie (though none of his favorite hot biscuits) and he accepted a piece.

Apparently pleased with his tour, Wright told us that if I arranged for someone to haul it in, he would provide his bulldozer and its driver to push the berm back up against the house. This was a welcome offer, not only saving some hundreds of dollars, but assuring that the berm would have correctly tapered lines at the ends of the house to harmonize with the architecture. (Just before winter I raked in a quantity of grass seed, including quite a bit of rye, which gave us a rich green cover on the new berm next spring.)

From that day on we received help and encouragement from Wright in finishing the house. In fact he became so proud of the house that he made it a test for some of his new clients: if they didn't like the Jacobs house, he turned them off! Although we continued friendly and close relations up to his death, and afterwards with the Taliesin Fellowship (which carries on the school and architectural enterprise started by Wright), I think I still retain some scar tissue, deep down, from the incident.

We put off the building of the two big flower boxes at the front of the house. We were pressed a bit for money by that time, and perhaps worn out with the strenuous spring and summer. Besides, Johnny Luginbuhl was tied up with other work. When we got around to building these flower boxes, the next spring, we found they truly were big—roughly six by seven feet each—and took several tons of stone; but Johnny, in just one long day, got them finished by sundown. As we stood back in the sunken garden and looked at them, we could see how they accented and completed the house, jutting out as they did to make a complete half-circle of the house masonry. By late spring, also, I had made screens for the doors and windows.

Two events in the fall of 1948 served to underline the importance of carrying out Wright's directions in full, just as the completion of the flower boxes a few months later would emphasize. The first event was aesthetic, involving a shelf about a foot below the balcony beams, which was to run the full sixty-foot length of the back wall, from the utility room's circular wall next to the fireplace. The low mezzanine ceiling, the curve of the wall, and the sudden lift of view from the edge of the balcony to the full fourteen-foot height of the glass doors, were all so spectacular and complete that I could see no need for such a long shelf. Then Wilfred Way installed the shelf, and we could see how it transformed the room, giving the continuity with its long line, and helping to create a sense of intimate space within this great expanse of living room, along with what seemed like particular space areas created by the curves of wall and windows. A contributing element, again, was the inch-and-a-half fascia strip at the front of the shelf, and we recalled how similar fascia strips on the shelves of the first house had transformed them from utilitarianism to an attractive architecture feature.

The other event was mechanical trouble which developed soon after we started the furnace in the fall. Hot water, forced by a pump, flowed through the pipes, but the water in the furnace gauge kept dropping. The steamfitter said soothingly that "the air" was "just getting out of the system." As the drop continued, I put my ear to the floor near one of the small "bleeder" valves which the steamfitter had insisted on installing, and heard a hissing, dripping sound. Wright's plans had not called for such valves. The small loop of copper pipe leading to the heating pipe had obviously been broken by the expanding and contracting pipes. The other three valve welds broke soon afterwards. I chopped a small hole in the concrete, found the leak by ear within

The carport stood next to the entrance driveway and served as a storage and drying area for wood cut from the three-acre woodlot at the right of the driveway. It was a long driveway to shovel. In later years a neighbor with his tractor kept the driveway plowed out in winter. (Photo by Herbert Jacobs)

an inch in each case, whittled wooden plugs, and told the steamfitter that since the bleeders were his idea, he could damn well shut them with new welds and repair the pipes and the holes in the floor. Being able to locate the leaks so easily reassured me in case of future leaks, but none ever appeared.

A roof for the carport next to the barn was the final outdoor project of the fall. In a November chill which nipped our fingers, one of Way's helpers, borrowed for half a day, lined up one rafter and the outside stringer for a roof cantilevered out from the low wall of stone that the masons had put up. I put in the rest of the rafters and covered them with roof boards and heavy tarpaper, providing shelter for two cars and a place to store the wood for our voracious fireplace.

The partitions for the row of four bedrooms on the mezzanine did not go nearly as fast, partly due to lack of time. My news writing class at the university naturally involved my spending a considerable amount of time correcting papers. In addition, I had become wire news editor of the paper, and I no longer had time at the office to write the daily column which I had started a few months earlier at the editor's request. Paid extra for the column, I wrote it at home, and soon found that I could produce three in one evening.

The partitions also went slowly because they approached cabinet work in requiring a good fit. The plans called for twelve-inch boards, put up at a forty-five degree slant, with a three-inch overlap. There was no studding, and each corner wrapped around a mezzanine support rod, thus requiring a slanting miter, which I found slow going without a miter box. At one exasperated moment I cried, "What I really need is a dressmaker!" By the time I got one bedroom partition up it showed my good intentions, and the rest were completed some weeks after Christmas. The entry to each bedroom was placed at a corner, giving more privacy—one could not see into the main part of the room as one walked past. Drapes were hung in all the bedroom doorways eventually. Wright's plan provided that the partitions stop at the bottom of the band of windows which circles the back wall under the roof. This left a triangular hole about three feet long, between the window ledge and the point where the slanting partition met the roof joist. It gave each bedroom a view out the windows of the adjoining rooms, as well as aiding air circulation, but did not offer a view into the interior of the adjoining rooms unless one made a real effort. For sensitive guests I made a triangular filler for this gap, but I think it was only called for once.

I was mildly concerned about the possible effect of those open triangles in the bedroom walls on the psyches of guests, but the children promptly found other uses for them. "Those unfilled triangles made wonderful opportunities for spying or practical jokes, as well as for quick conversations," Elizabeth recalled years later, "but we children quickly worked out the ground rules of privacy, since we were always potential recipients as well as jokers."

On a more serious note, Elizabeth now says, "My present love of carpentry goes back to the many hours of helping Daddy with various construction jobs, working up from soaping the screws and fetching tools to being entrusted with the brace and bit to screw in the screws which held the double-mitered partition

117

The mezzanine balcony walkway gave splendid views of the rolling countryside, as well as access to the bedrooms. The simple construction of the balcony parapet and the one-by-twelve reinforcing boards for the rafters show plainly. Below the balcony is the large hassock covered with sheepskins, a favorite for those who liked to stretch out before the fire. The ivy plant in the corner furnished an attractive addition to the stonework. (Photo © Ezra Stoller)

The slanting wall boards in the bedrooms, of one-by-twelve pine boards held together by a three-inch overlap, without studding, varied the horizontal pattern of the other woodwork. Entrances of four bedrooms, including the end one, appear here. The master bedroom is at the opposite end of the balcony. (Photo by Jack Steinberg)

As in the other bedrooms, a long shelf and built-in dressing table were featured in this guest bedroom. The triangular opening, which could be masked by branches or a temporary screen, permitted a view of more than one hundred and eighty degrees over the countryside. (Photo by Herbert Jacobs)

The end bedroom, with windows on three sides, was delightfully cool in summer, particularly because of the slot window at right, which usually stood open. At right is the mitered corner of the wall of the adjoining bedroom. (Photo © Ezra Stoller)

boards together in our bedrooms. Certainly the impetus and courage to build our own Taliesin house in the country (on a mountainside forty miles south of San Francisco) came from that wonderful building adventure.''

And how did the solar hemicycle cope with the wind? We remembered Wright's promise that with his design, ''an airfoil in place,'' with the sunken garden and the semi-circular shape of the house combining with the berm at the rear to cause the wind to blow over the house, rather than against it, ''you can light your pipe in front of the house even when there's a high wind.'' Yes, one could. We estimated that the airfoil effect cut the force of the wind at least in half, near the house. The berm sheltered the house from cold north winds, but most of our winter winds came from the southwest. Snow blowing toward us over the fields tended to drop and build up near the outer edge of the sunken garden.

The west end terrace, with stone walls on two sides and the big roof overhang, remained a year-round sheltered place, and even with patches of snow on the ground we could use it for sitting, or for taking a sunbath. The east terrace, because of the tunnel, was drafty. Wright's plans called for wind gates to be installed at the center of the tunnel, but I never built them. I tried an experiment with a couple of makeshift doors, but failed to anchor them solidly. When a strong wind dislodged them I did not try again, not being sure the results would be worth the effort.

We had almost daily evidence of winter solar heating. Usually by nine o'clock on a sunny morning, even in below-zero weather, the heating system stopped, and did not resume until late afternoon. The sun even reached the back wall below the mezzanine. The end piers and back wall formed what is now called a ''thermal mass'' (also referred to now as ''passive'' solar construction): they accumulated heat during sunny hours and gradually dissipated it at night. Of course the windows caused heavy heat loss at night, but this was partly offset by the drapes which Katherine made from a one-hundred-and-forty-yard bolt of natural-colored cabrillo weave cloth. Double glazing, or storm windows, would have made a material difference, but we did not feel that we had the money.

In summer the thermal mass had a reverse effect, cooling the house by absorbing excess heat during the day. The long slot

A fall of heavy, wet snow clings to the junipers of the flower box and the trees beyond, near the entrance to the house. Hanging from the roof is a ''stalk light,'' a favorite Taliesin illuminating decoration: a string of lights concealed by boxes and reflecting softly on horizontal boards. Eight-foot stalk lights hung in the two corners of the house. (Photo by Herbert Jacobs)

Masses of conifers, whose planting was specified by Wright, were developed at either end of the house, to help modify the severe winter winds. This snow scene, with little snow near the house, was typical of the winter landscape. Snow blew off the flat roof. Drained for the winter, the plunge pool supported a platform on which pine boughs were placed for decoration. (Photo by Herbert Jacobs)

Visitors approaching through the tunnel met this view of the sunken garden as they neared the corner of the house. Behind the trees and cornfield are the old farm buildings. (Photo by Herbert Jacobs)

window in the west pier and the smaller one in the kitchen stood open all summer, and with the bedroom windows, and appropriate open doors at the front, furnished plenty of air circulation. I did make a storm window for the west end slot window, since it was exposed directly to the west. John Sergeant, the British architect whose splendid book, *Frank Lloyd Wright's Usonian Houses,* featured both of our houses, stated that on his visit to the solar house, long after we had left it for California, he found that the thermal mass did not sufficiently cool the house. ("I found the solar gain excessive," he wrote.) I do not know whether the windows were opened as we had had them; and it is possible that he was not acclimated to a Midwestern summer.

Having wrestled for six years in the farm house with coal and oil stoves, we especially enjoyed the return to floor heating: feet and ankles always warm, air cool around the head, and no drafts. The mezzanine had no separate heating of its own, but the children and occasional guests never complained. In very cold weather we were apt to find ourselves dressing *en famille* in the big warm bathroom.

While finishing the interior we made a few minor changes without consulting Wright—who had already left for Arizona anyway. We did not put in the planned cupboards above the counter in the kitchen; we didn't have enough dishes to fill them, and besides, we liked the look of the bare stones. The bathroom was so large that I partitioned off a big closet for the master bedroom, with a door providing our own entrance to the bathroom.

I had firm ideas about the various chairs Wright had designed for other houses, and Wilfred Way relieved my guilt feelings when he estimated that the dining table chairs Wright had designed for us would cost over one hundred dollars apiece, because they required so many intricate cuts of wood. Instead we got on well with some cane-seated chairs that a Kentucky mountaineer industry produced for four dollars each. Their simple design blended in well. From Wright's designs I made five hassocks in one afternoon from the ends of partition boards, and Katherine made upholstered cushions for them. To the children's delight I also made one large hassock, later covered with sheepskins, for the corner by the fireplace, which turned out to be their favorite spot to sprawl or squirm on—depending on the interest of the tale—for their bedtime story.

With the entrance door at left, the panorama of both exterior and interior unrolled from the kitchen. At the right is the hexagonal table used by the family for breakfast, but the photographer has removed the dining table and chairs which stood behind it. I made the slant-sided hassocks from the scrap ends of bedroom partition boards. The fireplace is concealed by the curve of the wall which forms one side of the stairway to the mezzanine. (Photo © Ezra Stoller)

With the usual night lighting, the dining table and adjoining shelves as Wright designed them glow in natural wood colors. The shelves and cupboards below were scribed to fit against the stones, and complemented the hexagonal patterns of the dining table and the breakfast table in the foreground, which could be placed at the end of the dining table for additional seating. The lamp next to the easy chair at left was made from a leftover curved rib of the staircase interior wall. (Photo by Herbert Jacobs)

The long counter of the kitchen, with cupboards below, was sometimes crowded with dishes when meals for sixty or seventy were in preparation. Working drawings called for cupboards above the counter, but we preferred the view of the masonry and did not need the shelf space. The slot window, opening on the tunnel, provided plenty of ventilation and sometimes a preview of a visitor soon to appear at front door. (Photo by Herbert Jacobs)

The dining table in use for a family gathering in 1959. From the left are David J. Aitken, Elizabeth's brother-in-law; Byron (Bye) Baldridge, an old Aitken family friend; William, me, Susan and her former husband David Wheatley, and Katherine. A screen for the kitchen, made and painted by David Wheatley, appears in the background. (Photo by Herbert Jacobs)

A Christmas tree cut from our own lot and big enough to touch the ceiling finally achieved William's goal. Carrying some extra branches is Peter Coye, son of a neighbor. The farmhouse and barn we used for six years appear in the distance. (Photo by Katherine Jacobs)

When we came later to hear of Wright's occasional drastic reactions to changes clients made in their houses, we appreciated his tolerance and kindness toward our own delays and minor alterations. He was obviously pleased with our house, to the extent of making it a test for some clients; and he never once hinted, for instance, that with fifteen dollars for materials and a little effort on my part I could have taken less than ten years to build the elegant dining table he had designed, rather than the less suitable one at which he occasionally sat. I can well believe the statements of some writers and former Taliesin apprentices that Wright was deeply interested in ways of providing great housing for persons of modest means, and was willing to overlook inexpert work if they were doing it themselves. But while he did not press me to get on with the job, his mind was constantly at work, thinking of ways to improve the house. At one time he suggested an elaborate paneling between the beams of the mezzanine, to conceal the underside of the plank floor, but I shuddered at the amount of cutting and fitting involved.

With the rush of fat commissions after the war Wright had treated Taliesin to some elaborate rugs of his own design, which glorified the living room and loggia, and he suggested the same sort of rugs to cover the concrete floor in front of our fireplace. But I thought instead of my custom of bringing in the fireplace wood in the same wheelbarrow I had used to roll up construction stone, and of the comfort and ease with which I could do carpentry there with a quick cleanup by sweeping the leavings into the fire.

We scarcely even speculated on the pleasures of such amenities, just liking things as they were. We had embraced immediately the renewed joys of living in a Wright house. We experienced once

Illuminated chiefly by the fire, the family appears here beside the fireplace. We laid the half-circle of hearth stones and began using the fireplace even before the roof was built. The wooden boxes above shielded the living room lights. Basic wiring was in conduits against the wall at floor level in living room and mezzanine, with outlet plugs at intervals. Cables dropped to the box and grille lights. (Photo by Jack Steinberg)

again that feeling of the sense of space and shelter, the framing of attractive views by architecture, and the sense of garden and all outdoors forming part of the house.

The children also responded to the space and convenience. In summer they loved the plunge pool, the chance to tear madly around the sunken garden after the dog, toss a few frisbees, or just loaf in the sun, or in the shade of the corner roof overhangs. Inside there was the pool and its plants and fish in winter, an occasional frog or tree toad sitting at the edge, a school of polliwogs trying to escape the fish. We had Christmas trees cut from our own plantings, which finally touched the roof, the constant pleasure of a fireplace where one could build castles in the flames—and an equally satisfying joy: steaks from our own steers, broiled in the fireplace, with the extra flavoring produced by locust wood bark.

If we had guests, or a party, the children managed to put themselves to bed. They could, and often did, continue to take part as spectators, draping themselves over the balcony, watching and listening, until they got tired of it. They had the special advantage of the big windows, which acted as a giant mirror, permitting them to keep an eye on all the activity underneath the balcony.

The mezzanine balcony served as more than a spectator perch for the children at the parties of grown-ups. Elizabeth and William never tired of telling about the time they were alone in the house one afternoon when some visitors arrived unannounced and uninvited. The two children, more bored than their parents about visitors, decided to remain upstairs and see what happened. When the visitors got no answer to their knock, they simply walked in and toured the ground floor, commenting loudly on their likes and dislikes of the architecture. While the two youngsters suppressed giggles and held their breath, the intruders decided not to mount the stairs, and departed.

Although running on the balcony was strictly forbidden, ostensibly to avoid damage, but chiefly to safeguard the parents' ears from a fearful din, the children found it irresistible when the elders were absent. "When we were home alone, we had several lovely chase-games on that balcony, verifying Wright's excellent engineering," Elizabeth reported smugly many years later.

While I am not contending that we lived a life of nothing but merriment, we did relish what seemed like a great many awkward but hilarious moments. When we set out aquatic plants in boxes I made for the inside pool I thought it would be a splendid idea to throw a couple of shovelsful of dried cow manure into each box for fertilizer. But when the water rose, those hunks popped up from beneath the soil, and floated around the pool, just as some visitors appeared at the door. We made a mess trying through our laughs to get them buried again, but had to give up.

On another occasion, after a raucous session until three in the morning with an old friend and his new wife, with everyone trying to make selected portions of the truth prevail, I stepped out of the door the next morning with milk pail in hand on the way to the barn. I was a bit bleary-eyed, but with enough vision to perceive, even at eight o'clock, that Wright and those prestigious clients, the Harold Prices (of the family for whom the famous tower at Bartlesville and two houses would be built), had driven up, and were about to get out of their cars. Taken aback, I barely had time to slip into the house and shout an alarm to the solid sleepers, and then dash outside again to hold off the visitors while the commotion of cleaning up ashtrays and glasses and making of beds could be carried on. Since Wright had a subconscious feeling that he still was proprietor of all his houses, and the clients in them were rather like tenants, he never felt any necessity to give advance warning of his visits, no matter what the occasional trauma to the psyches of the occupants.

During one particularly snowy winter that built up a high bank of snow at the outer edge of the sunken garden, the children in a burst of energy produced about a dozen snowmen. We applauded their zeal, but when the snowmen gradually turned to ice, and the sun melted them oddly into Giacometti-like slender, semitransparent wraiths, they were disturbing to look at. Although the figures looked like a council of emaciated ghosts sitting in judgment on us, the children insisted that they remain, so we endured, but drew the drapes at dinner to shut them out.

Another winter, daughter Susan discovered that she had lost the diamond from her engagement ring, apparently outside the house, but we looked vainly in the snow. Two days later, as I wheeled a load of wood in the wheelbarrow toward the fireplace, and paused a moment at the front door, there was the glittering diamond, stuck in the tread of the barrow wheel. Luckily the wheel had stopped diamond-side up.

The only terrifying experience we had in the house was a three-day very strong wind, with gusts up to seventy miles an hour, which kept rattling the windows. We could actually see the six-by-nine-foot panes bending in or out in response to changes in wind pressure, and feel the wood frames give with the gusts. Outside, we could see the roof overhangs at either end of the house visibly fluttering. Fearing a sudden broken pane, we stayed back from the windows, but I got bored just watching and worrying, so I decided I might as well carry on my springtime job of fence repairing. I loaded a few fence posts onto the wheelbarrow and headed for the fields, but had to stop often to put the posts back on the barrow, because they blew off. I could plunge the posthole digger into the moist earth easily enough, but as the hole got deeper I found that it was oval-shaped because the wind pressed so hard against the blades of the digger. After three holes I quit, figuring that it was less wearing to sit inside with a book and listen to the wind. After the wind died down we discovered that our house was the only building in the area which did not suffer any damage. A large barn in a protected valley just a quarter of a mile away blew down. Other farms lost smaller buildings, and almost all had many shingles torn from roofs. (And many cars drove by slowly in the next two days, apparently so their owners could check on whether our house still stood.)

My somewhat dilatory efforts to finish up the last details of the building were interspersed with writing four books, continuing teaching, writing a daily column at home, and of course the usual forty hours-plus per week of reporting, editing and photography. The house gave me a second world to live in, a contrast to the sometimes demanding activities of the newspaper office. Without the stimulating change to that peaceful, aesthetic environment I might have found it more difficult to keep up that schedule. Each afternoon, driving back to the quiet of the country, and up through the trees to our secluded hilltop, and then walking into our own private world, with its sense of space and shelter embodied in stone and glass, revived and inspired me. I came each night to a house filled with activity—music, play, cooking and happy business in its various corners. And after dinner I would sit in the big chair near the glowing fireplace to read or write, in the midst of family activity. My books and all the fourteen years of daily columns were written here.

And outside the house was another enticing world to taste. For instance: whistling to the cardinal in the woods on a frosty winter morning to try to get him to answer before I reached the barn; giving a hand with the haying on a day off; taking down a big oak single-handedly for firewood, and persuading it to fall just where I planned; hoeing corn or potatoes or beans in the garden—all these were relaxers. But probably my greatest satisfaction came from the twice-a-day milking, a rhythmic, contemplative twenty minutes or so with my head against the warm and friendly cow—perhaps an early form of Transcendental Meditation—was a great source of inner joy. I had the reassuring knowledge that if I was really pressed for time, I could always get some other member of the family to do it; and there was a country saying which I occasionally put into practice: "It's a poor cow that won't hold two milkings."

From spring to brisk fall, the plunge pool was a twice-a-day refresher after milking. Since I made it a point of pride never to wear a suit in my own pool, you may well ask whether I was ever surprised in it. The first occasion was when the editor of the Middleton weekly paper came by to solicit renewal of my subscription. He was so abashed that he stayed at the corner of the house.

The second occasion was a bit racier. I was happily immersed, when an elegantly dressed woman suddenly appeared, walked up to the pool, introduced herself, and insisted on shaking hands. It turned out that she had come to Madison to take part in a symposium on Wright at which I was also to speak. She lived in the converted stable of an early Wright house in Chicago.

While I enjoyed my morning and evening dips in the plunge pool, the children probably got more solid pleasure out of it, and of course had many more hours available to use it. "That pool was a great addition," says Elizabeth. "It was plenty large for cooling off, horsing around, or lounging in the water. The absence of suits was an occasional source of amusement. We would beep a car horn or make some out-of-sight commotion to surprise a bather, sending him (or her) running for a towel only to discover it was a false alarm. Father was never sent into flight, however. He would only dress himself in his evening martini and look with interest toward the tunnel walkway."

18.

"There's Someone at the Door"

Visitors—bane or blessing? Well, mostly the latter, but our country location did not stop the steady flow of architects, students, prospective Wright clients, and the merely curious. In keeping with postwar prosperity, we soon boosted our rate to a dollar (fifty cents or free to architectural students) and it eventually more than paid for Wright's fee. We were as enthusiastic about this solar house as we had been about our first Wright house, so we did not try to turn people away.

How could you say no, for instance, to a fellow like Pierre Zolli, an engaging young heel-clicking Swiss architect, who had walked the eight miles from Madison in a blizzard? Or to friends who called asking whether they could bring out Niels Bohr, the famous Danish physicist, who proved architecturally appreciative and delightful?

Perhaps the outstanding example of persistence was Robert Muirhead, a Plato Center, Illinois corn farmer. He wanted a Wright house, but he wished to be sure that all his relatives would be happy about it too. Over a period of two years some twenty-five Muirhead relatives came by to have a look and ask questions. The verdict must have been favorable, because he was soon building. Wright suggested a rise in a field, the only elevation in the flat Illinois prairie bottom, as a site, which would have given a sort of masthead view over the waving corn tassels. But Muirhead was not about to cut into good cornland for such purposes. Wright had to settle for an orchard site, minus any distant view. We stopped on an eastern trip to visit the cohesive Muirhead family as they were almost ready to move into the new house. Muirhead was especially pleased that Wright had provided a place for him to work on his tractor close to the living room.

One Sunday noon, driving back from Madison, we met a motorist who asked if we could direct him to the Jacobs house. "Just follow me," I said, and thus we met the lively and entertaining Alfonso Iannelli, who had produced the sculptures for Wright's Midway Gardens in Chicago in 1914. His face, as he recounted anecdotes of Wright at the lunch table, struck us as itself highly sculptural.

Often our first glimpse of visitors was of figures walking boldly around the rim of the sunken garden, busily snapping pictures. This was the signal for one of us to step out, tell them there was a charge if they wanted to visit the house, and if not, "Be gone!" But they always came in, some to walk in stunned silence, jaws agape, others to gush, and some intolerables to try to tell us about other houses they had known. One girl, clutching her young man by the hand, was in and out in five minutes, uttering the single word "God!" every ten steps. The prize to me was a solemn youth who, when told that the house was not yet fully completed, glanced at the stonework and then said in all seriousness, "You know, you're going to have an awful time plastering these walls."

As with the first house, we were on "the Burnham list," the catalogue of Frank Lloyd Wright houses and their addresses in six Midwestern states, handed out by the Burnham Architectural Library of the Art Institute of Chicago. If we wanted a peaceful Sunday afternoon I would occasionally put a sign in the middle of the driveway: "The family is at prayers. Please do not disturb." I called that "practical religion."

Our very first party in the house, just a few days after the glass had been installed, mixed comedy, near-tragedy, and high finance, plus a strong dash of architectural advice. The late Gerald M. Loeb, leading light of the big Wall Street firm of E.F. Hutton and Company, wrote that he would like to talk to me on his way out to see Wright at Taliesin. I was familiar with the name, because Wright had told me a year or more earlier of Loeb's desire for a house, tempered by the cautious approach of a financier. When Wright first showed the design to Loeb, at that time unmarried, Wright had told him that he would fall in love with it, and as he spread out the drawings with a flourish Wright had declared, *There's* your bride!"

The circumspect Loeb, a director of New York's Museum of Modern Art, gave the museum five thousand dollars to produce a model of the house, so that he could see an in-the-flesh view of

Alfonso Iannelli, who in his mid-twenties sculptured the many stylized figures which graced Wright's Midway Gardens in Chicago, stopped by one Sunday noon to see the solar house. He is pictured here against the background of a Japanese sculpture at Taliesin at Wright's funeral in 1959. (Photo by Carmie A. Thompson)

what his bride would look like. He indicated in his letter to me that he wanted advice on the construction bids, and that he had married since the design had been completed. We invited the Loebs to dinner and also arranged a cocktail party beforehand, with Loeb's consent, which brought Madison's top financial people clamoring to attend, when the word got out that this top Wall Street figure would appear and perhaps disclose some inner secrets.

About fifteen of Madison's financial giants gathered, but being more interested in which way the stock market was going to go than in anything else, most gave only casual glances at the architecture. I was downstairs, listening to questions of the youngest of the guest financiers, who was more attracted by aesthetics than by Mammon. "Look at this!" he cried, pointing to the balcony and stonework as he walked rapidly along the windows, looking up and gesturing with his glass. Before I could warn him, he stepped right off into the air as he got to the inner pool, which at that time was still empty of water or plants. He suddenly lost altitude with the eighteen-inch drop, stumbled almost to horizontal, but kept going, glass still in hand and still gesturing, as he mounted the other side, still talking excitedly as he continued his tour. During all our time in the house, he was the only person who fell into either pool.

After the financiers had departed, Loeb got down to the business closest to his heart: how to cut the cost of his proposed house. The bids for this one bedroom creation had come in at around six hundred thousand dollars. "What can I do?" Loeb asked plaintively. "Mr. Wright thinks I am making much more money than is the fact." (Wright always seemed interested in "the constructive redistribution of wealth.") About all we could suggest, after a look at the plans and a long discussion, was that he appeal to Wright to think up ways of cutting the cost. I rightly

Tables in the sunken garden as well as inside, and the banks below the terrace, accommodated dozens of guests at dinner parties like this one held for colleagues in the office where Katherine worked. Japanese lanterns helped illuminate the scene, in a picture taken at dusk. (Photo by Herbert Jacobs)

guessed that Wright would not cut and Loeb would not build. During dinner Loeb pulled out pictures of the Connecticut house he was modernizing into an "interim bedroom," on which he had already spent twenty-two thousand dollars, he said.

We held a more rollicking type of party at the end of November for all the workmen and their wives. We had a gay time at dinner with the three masons and their wives, and then the others—about twenty-five in all—came in for a look around. Everyone seemed delighted to see the house glowing with warmth and light. Some of them confessed that they had wondered ahead of time whether the traditional "contractor's party" might end, as occasionally happened, with the owner's announcement that he was filing for bankruptcy before paying any bills. The Taliesinites had all headed for Arizona before this and we did not attempt a party for them that year, in spite of the exhilaration of being settled in the house.

The fact that the house lent itself so easily to large groups, plus our own pleasure in showing it off, combined to produce many notable gatherings as the years passed. At the end of the first holiday season in the new house we started to add up all those who had been entertained, such as the financiers and the Loebs, Middleton villagers, the workmen, the reporters' union, and others, and were amazed to find the total nearly four hundred.

Later, for sheer grace and beauty, I found nothing equalled the dinner before the high school prom for Susan and about seventy of her classmates. (Like the other two children who followed her, she attended the high school run in Madison in connection with the University, rather than the Middleton village high school.) The girls were delightedly at the age where nearly all of them could hold up a strapless gown, *de rigueur* in that era, and the boys, hair short and slicked down, appeared in a uniform of white jackets. And all responded to this lovely setting with their very

131

best manners. They sat at card tables scattered the length of the living room, and with candles on every table, and the reflections from the front windows, they made a charming picture. Fortunately for us, the passion for all-night parties purveyed by the parents, with the implied blackmail threat—"If you don't, some of us will go out and kill ourselves in cars"—had not yet raised its head.

The first party in the new house for Mr. and Mrs. Wright and the Taliesin Fellowship took place with warm and festive spirit in the fall of 1949; and all sixty or more guests arrived in the gala evening dress which they assumed for their own weekend social occasions. In Taliesin style, we had made the house attractive with many branches and fall flowers. We seated and served Mr. and Mrs. Wright in the big chairs next to a hexagon table, and served the other guests buffet style from the dining table, and they found their own seating on chair, couch, bench or hassock, with some on cushions on the floor.

A brief moment of drama came when Wright said to Katherine, "I think the drape over the pool should be shorter. Come here and I will show you. Bring scissors and we will fix them right now." Having spent a week making them, she had no intention of letting him wield the scissors. I was curious myself to see how the shorter length would look, but some of our old Taliesin friends, even while they held up the curtains to demonstrate the effect, looked worried. The shorter length seemed attractive, but we thought of their usefulness against sun and cold—and failed to produce the scissors. We reversed the usual entertainment procedure with this first Taliesin party in the new house, when Susan and a friend furnished the music (she was then at the concerto stage) rather than having the Taliesin chorus sing.

Another very special evening for us came in July, 1959 when the Taliesin Fellowship gave a dance and music recital at the University of Wisconsin, commemorating Mr. Wright, who had died in April of that year. Including Mrs. Wright, some hundred and twenty Taliesinites and their guests came to the house for an after-theater dinner. They made an attractive picture as they moved around in the lighted house and the terrace and sunken garden, which was decorated by strings of Japanese lanterns put up by William. Mrs. Wright's hand-written note said:

"Dear Mrs. Jacobs: Thank you for the lovely and colourful party. Please tell Bill his lanterns were beautifully distributed through the garden. It was most kind of you and Mr. Jacobs to take so much trouble to give us pleasure. Affectionately, Olgivanna Lloyd Wright."

The village of Middleton's curiosity about the house was mostly satisfied with a tea for some two hundred women from the Community Church, where Katherine had sung in the choir. We held several annual parties for members of the Newspaper Guild, usually with a large ham served buffet style, followed by a few work-related skits, and lots of dancing (great on that polished floor).

My only worry at all these gatherings was the mezzanine, and the tendency of too many plump persons to congregate on it in one spot, just above the indoor pool, to view the scene below and beneath them reflected in the windows. I had plenty of confidence in the steel rod holding up a ton or more of flesh, but I wasn't so sure about the strain on the rafter above, to which it was attached. However, the rafter never gave forth a crack or whimper, nor was there any cataclysmic plunge of humanity into the pool.

A writer for a popular women's magazine characterized one aspect of the house with a single sentence. She and a male companion had come up to look us over, to see if we were worthy of an illustrated feature article. They toured the premises, mostly in silence, and then the woman exclaimed, in tones of horror, "Why, you don't have a single thing in this house that we advertise!" They couched their "no" in fulsome thanks, but they must have considered us un-American, and traitors to Madison Avenue.

Their indictment was all too true. Except for the plain white refrigerator and stove, the dining chairs and the piano, everything from the kitchen cabinets to the long couch at the other end of the house had been built right on the premises. In its first years the couch cushion was even made of flour sacks stuffed with corn husks, to the annoyance of our daughters and other teenagers who enjoyed that hideaway. Everything else—music cabinet, tables, hassocks, easy chairs—had been made, and rather expert-

OLGIVANNA LLOYD WRIGHT

July 27 1969

Dear Mrs. Jacobs,

Thank you for the lovely and colourful party. Please tell Bill his lanterns were beautifully distributed through the garden.

It was most kind of you and Mrs. Jacobs to take so much trouble to give us pleasure

Affectionately

Olgivanna Lloyd Wright

Mrs. Wright's thank you letter for the after-theater dinner party given the Taliesin Fellowship and guests following a dance performance at the University of Wisconsin as a memorial to Mr. Wright. (Copyright © Olgivanna Lloyd Wright 1978)

ly, from wood and wood scraps. The dining utensils were my grandmother's wedding silver, dating from 1860.

Even the floor lamp beside my chair I had made from a leftover curve of two-by-four originally fashioned as part of the staircase partition. Wright, pleased at its looks, had urged me to patent the design. The floodlights overhead were porcelain sockets behind wooden grilles that I made. But everything looked at home, and fitted to its place.

Wright had designed a grille of two-by-fours next to the front door to partly screen the view of the kitchen, but we felt that it cut off too much light from the kitchen, and prevented a view of sunsets during half the year. Told of our doubts, Wright did not even urge us to complete his design by building it. "Live with the problem for a while, and see what you like," he suggested. He said it was like a robin building a nest—you did what seemed to work best. We tried a screen of reeds, woven by Katherine on a hanging loom that I made. That worked fairly well, but we ended with a folding wooden screen made by Susan and her husband and painted by them in an architectural design, which completely closed off the kitchen when we entertained, but could be folded to the wall at other times.

Upstairs it was the same story of "nothing to advertise." Except for the bathroom fixtures and the mattresses, everything—the shelves and dressing tables, the simple pallets holding the mattresses, even the elaborate cabinets and headboards of the master bedroom—had been built in place. The drapery which served as screen for the west end bedroom was an antique original from Kashmir, a heavily embroidered piece of fabric whose finely woven pattern caught light from behind and shone with jewel-like colors.

Both of our houses easily accommodated the furniture we made or acquired, such as the floor lamps, the transformed studio couch and the mountain crafts dining chairs. The only requirement seemed to be that they have simple design and harmonize with the low horizontal scale of the architecture.

19.

The Ripple Effect

Many of the visitors who came to look at Wright's designs and our living arrangements were prospective clients who came with problems or questions. The Usonian first house, with its well-publicized low price, attracted persons who were delighted to discover that Wright would design dwellings for clients of very moderate means. To see a house like that actually built and in use meant far more than looking at pictures and plans, and a score or more persons came, saw, and later built. The solar house attracted a much wider cross section—the moderate-cost enthusiasts, plus those who could afford a more elaborate house, and even a very light sprinkling of quite wealthy persons.

Because the house was so widely publicized, and was so near Taliesin, as well as being Wright's first post-war house to be built, many a prospective client dropped by to ask our help as persons who had been through the experience twice. Several came at Wright's suggestion. They wanted to know how we had managed to build two houses, how we kept costs down, and especially, "how was Wright to work with?" A very special couple were the Kenneth Laurents of Rockford, Illinois, who stopped by two or three times. Mr. Laurent was confined to a wheelchair, and Wright designed a semi-circular house for them that was somewhat like ours.

Now and then we had what I called "closet clients," familiar to architects as persons who go from one architect to another, accumulating sets of plans, but even when they have achieved a closet full never quite bringing themselves to the final step of starting to build. Many of our other visitors did build, and in later years we would get a Christmas card or letter, proudly enclosing a snapshot of a completed house.

A project closer to home than most was that of the First Unitarian Society of Madison, which had sold its downtown building for a good round sum, and had engaged Wright, a member since his youthful Madison days, to design a new meeting house. The small membership, down to a few score at one time, had labored for a year trucking stone from a quarry, and had seen the dramatic shell of the building rise to a point where the money was gone and the building still incomplete. They had signed a cost-plus contract, and were now disheartened. First mention of the church came in September, 1950 in my Garden Book, when I recorded that Katherine had had members of the Women's Alliance of the church out for tea and had talked to them "regarding the building of the church and their part in it," sharing our experience in an effort to encourage them.

We visited the church, were disturbed by its incomplete appearance, and soon found ourselves as members. Wright was attempting to spur action, because the building presented a sad advertisement for his architecture in its present state. Much of the ceiling plastering, inside and out, had not been done, a rough plywood partition closed off the main assembly room, the congregation sat on rickety old funeral parlor chairs, and the Sunday School wing was unfinished, among other things.

To get them going, Taliesin had designed an elaborate drape more than a hundred feet long, to replace the plywood partition to the main room. Mrs. Wright sent in two Taliesin looms, one of which went to our house, and the women of the church began weaving. Taliesin had furnished an elaborate pattern, and Katherine worked out drawings of blocks of color from the sketches, for each panel. In the early summer of 1951 Wright made a bold proposal, promising to send in the entire Taliesin Fellowship for a month to plaster walls and ceiling, make pews, paint, landscape the surroundings, and put the whole building in shape. He himself would give three talks at the church to raise money. He had already waived his architectural fee. His only condition was that Katherine be put in sole charge of all the activities. She had become a member of the board of directors.

The race against time was the sort of challenge that Taliesin relished and usually won. Wright's bulldozer, piloted by William Wesley Peters, tore up the land; a power saw screamed in the big assembly room, making plywood into pews and tables; plaster and paint flew. People set up cutting tables and sewing machines to make the endless drapes and cover cushions. Church members cooked, sewed, and painted. Many ravaged their gardens to furnish a lunch each noon for the work crew. Katherine found it thrilling to be part of that drive and dedication in bringing out the beauty of the building. The young Taliesinites worked early and late, the last couple of days all night through, to finish the building in time for Wright's lectures. When they got too tired they would stop and sing Palestrina hymns, or some of the many songs in the Taliesin chorus repertoire, and then go back to work. We were away from home so much during that month that a skunk took up residence in the flowerbox next to the front door, but decided to leave when we resumed our life at home.

I even got into the construction act myself, in a typical last-minute Taliesin cliffhanger. Wright had spotted a big window in the church's assembly room, and decided that its framing was not what he wanted. He drew a new design, ordered the old frame torn out, and was standing with me at the empty frame an hour before he was to begin the lecture series in the church before five hundred people. With Wright's usual luck, a truck with the needed glass rolled up at that moment. While Wright shouted orders, the truck driver and I lifted that heavy piece of plate glass into place and held it while Wright tacked on cleats to hold it there. But Wright wasn't finished. His eye fell on two large narrow rolls of carpeting. "Herbert!" he said imperiously. "Roll out those carpets. I'll show you where." So I obediently rolled them out along the central axis of the church. In fact, I laid one of them twice, because the first time I got it upside down. With these runners laid to his satisfaction, Wright said triumphantly, "There's your church"—and he was right. The carpets gave the final touch needed to pull the whole thing together, leading the eye down the long corridor adjoining the assembly room and giving a sense of space to the building.

Katherine introduced Wright to two overflow audiences which brought in over a thousand dollars, and Wright wandered about the room as he spoke demonstrating the acoustics—and praising the architecture. The church debt, for plywood, cushions, gold cloth drapes, plastering the ceiling and painting, finishing the front office, and other matters, rose by some thirty thousand dollars. But the church was now complete, a going concern, and zooming membership and finances soon made it a success.

Many of the new members, who had not been "present at the creation," had a lot of questions. As unofficial church flack, I sent a list of them to Wright, providing space between them for answers. These were as provocative as usual. As to why the Sunday School room windows were too high to look out of, Wright wrote that the children were there to learn, not look, and "the little beggars do not appreciate landscape even if there was one." But the low windows in the main assembly room, he explained, were "to look out of, in case the congregation gets bored looking at the preacher." The church is designed with its main rooms, floor pattern and other architectural features on a triangular pattern, but Wright always denied to me, with a straight face, that he was perpetrating an architectural pun on the Unitarians, who have their doubts about divinity and Trinity. He insisted that the roof over the celebrated "prow" of the church was "like hands raised in prayer,"—also a concept alien to the membership.

Although I never rose above a brief committee chairmanship in the church hierarchy, I did serve on the pulpit committee to recommend a new minister. We were looking for someone who would take on that small group of loyal Unitarians and their new, dramatic building—and found him: the Rev. Max D. Gaebler. He officiated at Wright's funeral, and has been with the church now for more than twenty-five years. He also conducted the marriage services in the church for both our daughters. Twice I myself presided at Sunday services where Wright was the speaker, one of them being an occasion when he was a full half hour late; even the organist had given up on trying to fill in, when Wright finally strolled in.

Another Wright proposal that kept me occasionally involved for twenty-three years, until I left the paper, was the Monona Terrace Project, an elaborate civic center complex of steel and concrete to be built at the edge of Lake Monona, two blocks from the state capitol, to provide city and county offices and courts, a large theater, and other rooms. He sprang this idea in 1938, exclusively in our paper—which may have queered it right there, since the editor had stepped on many toes. I wrote the story and cutlines for the drawings. Two years later Wright presented the idea to the county board in an emotional speech, but the board turned it down. (In one of his Princeton lectures in the early Thirties, Wright had made the prophetic statement that "when the artist

Frank Lloyd Wright appears here in the pulpit as speaker at Sunday services in the Madison Unitarian Church, which he designed in the mid-forties. He had been a member since his boyhood in Madison some seventy-five years earlier. When the spectacular building was completed in 1951 with the aid of a work crew from Taliesin, it attracted many new members. (Photo by Herbert Jacobs)

goes out into the street" to solicit clients he is apt to be viewed with suspicion, and this burden was always carried by the project.)

After World War II the city and county built jointly what Wright scoffed at as "a caved-in shoebox," but shortly afterward the Monona Terrace project was revived as a theater, convention hall, and art and drama center. In a city referendum voters approved a theater-auditorium and Wright as architect. (I always thought it a compliment to the city that a majority came down on the right side in an aesthetic matter.)

Opponents delayed matters skillfully, and even got a state law passed to block the whole idea. Delays, plus added features which opponents wormed into the project, boosted the cost from four million to a whopping thirteen million dollars, at which voters balked. Although the regular city hall reporters generally covered the project, I got a call from Wright one night at ten-thirty, asking that I rush into the hotel and interview him, just after he had had a knock-down fight with the city council over his contract. Katherine and I had been in the midst of mortaring-in some stones, raising the hearth three inches to cure a smoke problem. (It did, but she was left with the task of finishing the job, and cleaning up.) By the time I finished the interview it was nearly one a.m. and my car, stuck in a snowbank, needed help from the mighty arm of Wesley Peters.

On many other occasions I was called to the editor's office to listen to doleful harangues every time Wright brought in another of the articles he wrote on economic or political questions, issues far afield from architecture. Wright dominated the editor, who got his reward in being on a first-name basis with a person of international renown, but always there were the ritual groans to me first from the editorial sanctum, beginning "Now here's another of those articles . . . ."

Much more pleasurable associations with Taliesin for us at this time than the doomed Monona Terrace project were the special parties and the Wright birthday celebrations—to all of which we were invited—when the rush of clients after World War II brought Wright plenty of money for the first time in his life. The special parties were held on summer evenings, partly to entertain current and prospective wealthy clients, partly to give the appren-

tices an opportunity to develop their creative skills in skits and costumes, in decorating, and in cooking and serving a meal attractively. One lively party was billed as a Showboat, with Mr. and Mrs. Wright and some of the guests arriving by stagecoach, and some on horseback, many in costume. They were seated at vine- and flower-decorated tables in the big drafting room. Wesley Peters had painted an elaborate showboat stage curtain, and the program included a hilarious shootout with pistol blanks and running dialogue between Peters and the Wrights' daughter Iovanna. Wright and his wife seemed to outdo the guests in laughter and enjoyment on these occasions.

A more elaborate production was a fourteenth century Italian scene: Marco Polo returning to Venice, with a retinue of lovely ladies and musicians, who stepped from a miniature Venetian galleon built by the apprentices. Marco Polo handed out gifts from a treasure chest to the guests, who sat under a canopy of streamers. That year a real Italian prince was a member of the Fellowship, and had a part in the performance.

Once a year, Wright, then in his mid-eighties, addressed a jam-packed audience of University of Wisconsin students, who adored this quintessential rebel's standard speech on the futility of a formal education. (Wright stated in his autobiography that he attended the University of Wisconsin for three and a half years, but the university's official records indicate only a few months' attendance.) The architect, dressed all in black, his mass of white hair brushed carefully back at the sides, always made a dramatic entrance, sauntering slowly from the wings toward the lectern. On these occasions he liked to wear a ribbon around his neck with a gold medal dangling from it, given to him in Florence in 1951. "The de Medici medal, the one Dante coveted, but never got," I heard him murmur proudly on another occasion.

His sharp tongue and harsh comments on fellow architects had softened into a mellow, genial personality by this time. This was notable in the public celebration of his birthdays, which began rather modestly in 1953 with just sixteen outside guests, from Spring Green, Madison, and other Wisconsin places, including four members of our family who gathered for the June 8th celebration. The party grew the next year, and in two years had become a glittering extravaganza with as many as a hundred

Gaily costumed Taliesin apprentices put on a fourteenth century Italian party for dozens of guests seated at small tables beside the Taliesin lake. Here Iovanna, the Wrights' daughter, hands out presents to the ladies, after "Marco Polo" has landed from a Venetian galleon built for the festival. Mr. and Mrs. Wright are seated at far right. (Photo by Herbert Jacobs)

The first of Wright's June 8 birthday parties to include guests from outside of Taliesin took place in 1953, and drew a handful of persons from nearby Wisconsin towns. The parties rapidly grew into extravaganzas with up to a hundred guests from both coasts and points in between. Seated here from left are William Jacobs; Mrs. Harold Groves, Madison; Marion Kanouse, Spring Green banker; Mrs. William T. Evjue, Madison; Mr. and Mrs. Wright; William T. Evjue, editor-publisher of the *Capital Times*; Susan and Katherine Jacobs; and Mrs. Richard Smith, Jefferson, Wisconsin, whose Wright house had recently been completed. Standing with me are Mr. and Mrs. Roger Schwenn, Madison, for whom Wright was designing a house, and Harold Groves, who represented the congregation of the new Unitarian church which Wright had designed. (Photo by James Roy Miller)

138

With his customary cane, porkpie hat and linen suit, Frank Lloyd Wright (center) mingled with some of the eighty guests who gathered for the traditional Taliesin West Easter breakfast in 1959. Wright, in expansive mood, had a quip or friendly greeting for everyone. The umbrellas shielded the most noted guests from the Arizona sun. (Photo by Herbert Jacobs)

guests, who flew in from New York, California, Arizona and Chicago. The parties became somewhat congested scenes, reported on the national news wires, for Wright had by then become an enthusiastic television personality, sometimes making half a dozen appearances in a week during a visit to New York. I attended these fetes both as guest and reporter, sometimes with a cameraman, sometimes taking the pictures myself when the newspaper felt impoverished—and boasting that I was the only person attending who was getting overtime pay for socializing.

The Easter breakfasts at Taliesin West, near Scottsdale, Arizona, were the other great festival occasions for Taliesin. Katherine, our son William and I drove out there for the one held March 29, 1959. Daughter Elizabeth was away at college, and Susan had joined the fellowship with her architect husband in the fall of 1958, and was already at Taliesin. The Wrights had often invited us, but we had never been able to get away at Easter, until that year of great snowbanks. We were housed in a small double tent, like those of many of the apprentices, and felt ourselves to be virtually part of the Fellowship.

We arrived after dark on Easter eve, so the next morning gave me my first clear view of Taliesin West and its celebrated desert masonry and canvas roofs, in a desert setting equally unfamiliar to me. I had no time to gawk, however, because my editor, an Easter guest, was on my neck immediately. This was the first time he had had a hired hand there to receive orders, and he was not about to waste a minute of my time. I was kept busy photographing all aspects of the scene, and in the afternoon rushed the negatives and a story to a plane going toward Madison, to fill a lot of the front page of the paper.

The sixty-odd guests, and an equal number of Taliesinites,

After the Easter breakfast, Mr. and Mrs. Wright posed patiently for the cameras of many guests. Mrs. Wright was resplendent in a bright red hat, and Wright showed no signs of the illness which was to bring his death less than two weeks later. A few minutes after the photographic session Wright waved his cane, said, "Come along, Mother" to his wife, and set off jauntily for a walk around the grounds. (Photo by Herbert Jacobs)

milled around a long L-shaped table, admiring decorations and each other, before we sat down. Most of the ladies, following a Taliesin tradition, were in wildly fanciful hats. I photographed Wright in the center of the group, near Harold Price, for whom he had designed the spectacular Price tower in Bartlesville, Oklahoma, and for whom he was currently doing a large house in Phoenix. Wright spotted Harold's bright blue suit, and I heard him sing out, "Harold, how did I happen to leave you enough money to buy a new suit? I must have overlooked something."

But within ten days of that joyous Easter celebration Wright died, aged ninety-one. I had returned to the office just in time to write his obituary. Actually, I had already written most of it. Dining with him the previous fall, I had been struck for the first time by how old he looked. During spare moments of the ensuing winter I had revised and added to the advance obituary material on notable personalities that the wire services make available to their media clients. To my dismay, the material had mostly emphasized the lurid incidents of Wright's domestic difficulties, with almost nothing on the man himself, his vast amount of work, his outstanding examples of buildings in all eight fields of architecture, his impact internationally as well as nationally during his seventy years of practice.

During the few days' interval between Wright's being taken to a Phoenix hospital and his death I was able to refine and cut the roughly forty pages I had accumulated, and it was promptly put into type. I was flattered to learn later that the editor had made my version available, at their request, to the wire services and several leading newspapers which were aware that our paper had always followed Wright closely.

Shortly after Wright's death I received a postcard, with a request for copies of the paper, from the late Charles "Fritz" Manson, who got his Wright house in 1940, after seeing ours, and had become our friend. He caught very well the blithe spirit that those who knew Wright treasure, along with Wright's deep concern for his profession, and for his clients, small as well as large. Manson expressed himself in a quizzical manner that Wright himself would have been the first to enjoy, voicing the respect and admiration, somewhat tinged with wonder and a touch of awe, that friends of Wright felt. He wrote: "I know we all have to die sometime, but I was beginning to think the old boy had talked God out of it."

Wright's coffin, in a farm wagon draped with pine boughs, was followed by mourners led by Mrs. Wright and Iovanna, who walked the half-mile to the Lloyd Jones chapel and burying ground. In the background are the buildings of Taliesin. William Wesley Peters, Wright's son-in-law, drove the wagon, used in earlier Taliesin funerals. At his side is Eugene Masselink, long-time secretary of Wright and of the Taliesin Fellowship, who read Wright's "Work Song" at the graveside. Walking beside the wagon is Richard Carney, Taliesin apprentice and Wright's driver for many years. (Photo by Carmie A. Thompson)

Even before Wright's death our own lives had begun to change. Susan was the first to marry and depart. Years later she and her husband, Kenneth Lockhart, built their own small and attractive house at Taliesin West. She has recently added piano solos and the production of graphics to her many skills.

Elizabeth married Donald Aitken in the spring of 1958, and after a year of study at the Max Planck Institute in Goettingen, Germany, they established themselves in California, where they soon built their own Taliesin-designed house. Their mountainside pastured a small flock of goats for the mohair which Elizabeth spun and wove, an art she taught her two daughters.

William entered Reed college, in Portland, Oregon, in the fall of 1961, going on to earn a doctorate in physics at the University of Washington and enter the absorbing life of an atomic researcher. His talented wife Natasha is a researcher in the history of science.

And that left Katherine and me alone in a house that seemed even bigger, now that it was so empty of activity, for Katherine herself had taken an engrossing job with a state agency. On occasional walks through residential streets of Madison we were depressed by the sight of many houses as large as our own which seemed merely to be decaying shelters for one or two oldsters living on memories and the hopes of visits from children or grandchildren.

We decided that our own house deserved to be filled and fully utilized by a young and growing family, rather than standing empty most of the day. When Katherine located a young professor and his wife who were coming to Madison with their five children, we promptly sold the house to them, hoping to see it pass into the care of loving hands, rather than waiting for someone willing to pay the highest possible price. We had followed the same practice in selling the first house.

At almost the same time, feeling less than enthusiastic about some of the new executives coming up on the paper, I accepted an offer to join the faculty at the University of California at Berkeley as a full-time journalism teacher, which seemed like a good new challenge in an excellent new place. We now live in a small house designed by Roger Lee with a pleasant "open plan" much in the spirit of Wright.

While I will concede that a certain ruggedness of disposition helped in building with Wright, when we look back on it all we can well echo this view of Elizabeth's: "The close participation in all parts of the building process was a wonderful enabling experience. My early lessons that 'all things are possible' taught me that the process of making them possible is not mysterious, though it is often difficult or even tedious, and it is always rewarding."

We "stayed the course," as Wright thought we might. And if we could break more architectural barriers with Frank Lloyd Wright, we would do it all again.

List of Illustrations

Index

The text and cover of this book were designed by
Wendy Cunkle Calmenson. Type was set by
Media Etcetera, Inc., in Times Roman and Gill Sans
Light. The book was printed and bound in Salt Lake City
at Publishers Press.